Chapter - 1   Introduction

Chapter - 2   Dirty Bomb

Chapter - 3   Nuclear Detterence

Chapter - 4   Nuclear Testing

Chapter - 5   Peaceful use of nuclear energy

Chapter - 6   CTBT

Chapter - 1

Introduction

The **Treaty on the Non-Proliferation of Nuclear Weapons**, commonly known as the **Non-Proliferation Treaty** or **NPT**, is an international treaty whose objective is to prevent the spread of nuclear weapons and weapons technology, to promote cooperation in the peaceful uses of nuclear energy and to further the goal of achieving nuclear disarmament and general and complete disarmament.[1]

Opened for signature in 1968, the Treaty entered into force in 1970. On 11 May 1995, the Treaty was extended indefinitely. More countries have adhered to the NPT than any other arms limitation and disarmament agreement, a testament to the Treaty's significance.[1] A total of 190 states have joined the Treaty, though North Korea, which acceded to the NPT in 1985 but never came into compliance, announced its withdrawal in 2003.[2] Four UN member states have never joined the NPT: India, Israel, Pakistan and South Sudan.

The treaty recognizes five states as nuclear-weapon states: the United States, Russia, the United Kingdom, France, and China (also the five permanent members of the United Nations Security Council). Four other states are known or believed to possess nuclear weapons: India, Pakistan and North Korea have openly tested and declared that they possess nuclear weapons, while Israel has had a policy of opacity regarding its nuclear weapons program.

The NPT consists of a preamble and eleven articles. Although the concept of "pillars" is not expressed anywhere in the NPT, the treaty is nevertheless sometimes interpreted as a *three-pillar* system, with an implicit balance among them:

- non-proliferation,
- disarmament, and
- the right to peacefully use nuclear technology.[3]

The NPT is often seen to be based on a central bargain: "the NPT non-nuclear-weapon states agree never to acquire nuclear weapons and the NPT nuclear-weapon states in exchange agree to share the benefits of peaceful nuclear technology and to pursue nuclear disarmament aimed at the ultimate elimination of their nuclear arsenals".[4] The treaty is reviewed every five years in meetings called Review Conferences of the Parties to the Treaty of Non-Proliferation of Nuclear Weapons. Even though the treaty was originally conceived with a limited duration of 25 years, the signing parties decided, by consensus, to extend the treaty indefinitely and without conditions during the Review Conference in New York City on 11 May 1995, culminating successful U.S. government efforts led by Ambassador Thomas Graham Jr..

At the time the NPT was proposed, there were predictions of 25–30 nuclear weapon states within 20 years. Instead, over forty years later, five states are not parties to the NPT, and they include the only four additional states believed to possess nuclear weapons.[4] Several additional measures have been adopted to strengthen the NPT and the broader nuclear nonproliferation regime and make it difficult for states to acquire the capability to produce nuclear weapons, including the export controls of the Nuclear Suppliers Group and the enhanced verification measures of the IAEA Additional Protocol

The Comprehensive Nuclear-Test-Ban Treaty: Helping to create a truly global community

by Mikhail Gorbachev
Former leader of the Soviet Union

When President Barack Obama signed the U.S. instrument of ratification for the new Strategic Arms Reduction Treaty, or START, on 2 February 2011, he cleared the way for the United States and Russia to put the landmark accord into effect. Three days later, the new START officially entered into force.

The new START reduces the size of the American and Russian nuclear stockpiles, thus representing a serious step forward for both countries. I hope this will energize efforts to take the next step to a world free of nuclear weapons: a ban on all nuclear testing.

In the final stretch, President Obama put his credibility and political capital on the line to achieve ratification. That a sufficient number of Republican senators put the interests of their nation's security, and the world's, above party politics is encouraging.

The success was not without cost. In return for the treaty's ratification, Mr. Obama has promised to allocate U.S.$ 85 billion over the next 10 years for modernizing the American nuclear weapons arsenal, which is hardly compatible with a nuclear-free world.

A total ban on nuclear explosions is of paramount importance

The priority now is to ratify the separate treaty banning nuclear testing. The stalemate on this agreement, the

Comprehensive Nuclear-Test-Ban Treaty (CTBT), has lasted more than a decade. I recall how hard it was in the second half of the 1980s to start moving in this direction. At the time, the Soviet Union declared a unilateral moratorium on nuclear testing. However, when the United States continued to test, we had to respond. Even so, we insisted on our position of principle, calling for a total ban on nuclear testing under strict international control, including the use of seismic monitoring and on-site inspections.

In 1996 the United Nations General Assembly finally opened the CTBT for signing and ratification. But this pact has a particularly stringent requirement for its entry into force: every one of the 44 "nuclear technology holder states" must sign and ratify it.

As of today, 35 have done so, including Russia, France and Britain. Still, the list of countries that have not ratified remains formidable: It includes the United

States, China, Egypt, Indonesia, Iran, Israel, India, North Korea and Pakistan (the final three have not even signed). Each "rejectionist" country has its arguments, but all are not equally responsible for the stalemate. The process of ratification stalled after the United States Senate voted in 1999 to reject the Treaty, claiming that it was not verifiable and citing the need

> »Universal ratification of the test ban treaty would be a step toward creating a truly global community of nations, in which all share the responsibility for humankind's future.«

for "stockpile stewardship" to assure the reliability of American weapons. The real reason was doubtless the senators' desire to keep testing.

Nevertheless, in the 21st century only one country, North Korea, has ventured to conduct nuclear explosions. There is, in effect, a multilateral moratorium on testing. It is increasingly obvious that for the international community nuclear explosions are unacceptable.

CTBT Verification regime can also help with disaster mitigation

In the meantime the Preparatory Commission for the Comprehensive Nuclear-Test-Ban Treaty Organization (CTBTO) has built up a strong verification regime. Over 260 monitoring stations — around 80 percent of the number needed to complete the system — are now fully operational. The system proved its effectiveness by detecting the relatively low-yield nuclear explosions conducted by North Korea in 2006 and 2009. And in March 2011, the system once again demonstrated its capability after the 9.0 magnitude earthquake off the coast of Japan triggered a massive tsunami. Data from the CTBTO's monitoring stations helped tsunami warning centres in Japan and the wider Pacific region to issue rapid tsunami alerts. Following the accident at the Fukushima Daiichi nuclear power plant, the CTBTO became an authoritative source of information on radiation dispersal around the globe for both its Member States and international organizations involved in nuclear safety and disaster mitigation.

So with North Korea being the only country to have conducted any tests over the last decade, should we, perhaps, be content with this virtual moratorium on nuclear testing?

No, because commitments that are not legally binding can easily be violated. This would render futile any attempts to influence the behaviour of countries that have been causing so many headaches for the United States and other nations.

U.S. Senate would be wrong to reject CTBT again

The American senators should give this serious thought. As George Shultz, Secretary of State under President Ronald Reagan, has said, Republicans may have been right when they rejected the Treaty in 1999, but they would be wrong to do so again.

It is fairly certain that once the Senate has agreed to ratification, most of the countries still waiting will follow. No country wants to be a "rogue nation" forever, and we have seen that dialogue with even the most recalcitrant governments is possible. Yet dialogue can work only if the United States refrains from telling others what they must not do while keeping its own options open.

On 23 September, foreign ministers from the CTBTO's 182 Member States will gather in New York for the

Conference on Facilitating the Entry into Force of the CTBT. They will jointly call upon those States that need to adhere to the Treaty so that it can enter into force. They will commit their countries to act at the highest political level to make this happen. Let's hope that this will lead to further ratifications, especially by the 'rejectionist' countries mentioned above. Universal ratification of the test ban treaty would be a step toward creating a truly global community of nations, in which all share the responsibility for humankind's future.

A version of this op-ed appeared in print on 29 December 2010 on page A23 of the New York Times.

Mikhail Gorbachev
was the last head of state of the Soviet Union. From 1985, he embarked on a programme of political, economic, and social liberalization under the slogans of *glasnost* (openness) and *perestroika*

(restructuring). He declared a moratorium on nuclear testing from 1985-87 and then again from 1991. While in power, agreement was reached with the United States on the Intermediate-Range Nuclear Forces Treaty in 1987 and START in 1991. In recognition of his outstanding services as a reformer and world political leader, Gorbachev was awarded the Nobel

the Comprehensive Nuclear-Test-Ban Treaty (CTBT)

Printed in Austria
July 2010
CTBT/LEGREL/LS/2

Contents

1. Basic obligations... 2
2. Why ratify the CTBT?... 3
3. Scope of the CTBT.. 6
4. History and significance of the CTBT...................... 7
5. Membership benefits.. 8
6. National implementation measures......................... 10
7. The National Authority... 12

8. Checklist for legislators.. 14
9. Ratifying States 16
10. Signatory States which have not yet ratified........... 17
11. Non-signatory States 18
12. Entry into force... 18
13. Resolutions by the Inter-Parliamentary Union........ 18

Background Information for Parliamentarians on THE CTBT

2

1. Basic obligations

ARTICLE I

1. Each State Party undertakes not to carry out any nuclear weapon test explosion or any other nuclear explosion, and to prohibit and prevent any such nuclear explosion at any place under its jurisdiction or

control.

2. Each State Party undertakes, furthermore, to refrain from causing, encouraging, or in any way participating in the carrying out of any nuclear weapon test explosion or any other nuclear explosion.

3

2. Why ratify the CTBT?

The aim of the Comprehensive Nuclear-Test-Ban Treaty (CTBT) is to end all nuclear weapon test explosions and any other nuclear explosion in an effectively verifiable manner. Over 2000 tests were conducted during the period 1945 to 1996. Only a few have occurred after 1996 — the year the CTBT was adopted by the United Nations General Assembly and opened for signature. Each and every signature

or ratification strengthens the political value of the
Treaty. Even without having entered into force, the CTBT
has helped to create a strong international norm against
nuclear weapon testing.

A nuclear test provides the final and irreversible 'downstream'
proof of the intentions of a State regarding its
pursuit of nuclear energy for peaceful or for weapons purposes.
The CTBT constitutes, thus, this last and clearly
visible barrier between the peaceful legitimate use and the
misuse of nuclear energy. This legal line needs to be drawn
firmly and irrevocably.

The CTBT is also a key to easing the rancour between the nuclear haves and have-nots. It is a strong non-proliferation instrument, a catalyst for nuclear disarmament, and crucial in a world in which we see the resurgence of nuclear energy. Preparations for entry into force of the Treaty are well under way by the CTBTO Preparatory Commission, with more than 84% of the International Monitoring System stations (seismic, hydroacoustic, infrasound, radionuclide) installed. States Signatories are equally entitled to all the benefits of the system. The wealth of data provided by the monitoring system has a variety of potential and important

civil and scientific applications as well, notably the contribution
to tsunami warning centres.
The nuclear weapon tests of 2006 and 2009, claimed by the
Democratic People's Republic of Korea, posed a challenge
to the Treaty and the Preparatory Commission on several
fronts. These events constituted the most serious trial
to the norm against nuclear testing for many years. International
condemnation of these events demonstrated the
seriousness of the international community to uphold the
global nuclear test ban. These events also imposed performance
tests for our organization and its nascent verification
regime. Although not all stations have been established or

are transmitting data yet, the verification regime nevertheless
functioned as a system, in a holistic and synergistic
way. Regrettable and disquieting as those events were, the
verification system's timely, integrated and coherent performance
demonstrated a high level of reliability. The system has proven to be a valuable investment by the States
Signatories to ensure that no nuclear test goes undetected.

Background Information for Parliamentarians on THE CTBT
The importance of universalization and the urgent entry
into force of the CTBT has been widely recognized by the
international community. This has been evidenced most
recently through the overwhelming support for the CTBT

at the United Nations General Assembly, in the Security Council and at the 2010 Review Conference of the Parties to the Treaty on the Non-Proliferation of Nuclear Weapons (NPT).

The time has come for the CTBT to enter into force. The opportunity is there and we must respond. We need to work together to make the world a safer place. For our own sake and for the generations to come.

Tibor Tóth
Executive Secretary
Preparatory Commission for the Comprehensive Nuclear-Test-Ban Treaty Organization
Vienna, June 2010

3. Scope of the CTBT

The object and purpose of the CTBT is to ban comprehensively nuclear weapon test explosions and any other nuclear explosion in any environment in an effectively verifiable manner. The CTBT aims at eliminating nuclear weapons by constraining the development and qualitative improvement of new or more advanced nuclear weapons. It plays a crucial role in the prevention of nuclear proliferation and in nuclear disarmament, thus contributing to a safer and more secure world.

When the Treaty enters into force it will establish a treatyimplementing body (the Comprehensive Nuclear-Test-Ban Treaty Organization (CTBTO)), including an on-site inspection mechanism and confidence-building measures as well

as an International Monitoring System (IMS) and International
Data Centre (IDC). The IMS and IDC are already being created and are being provisionally operated during
the preparatory phase by the Preparatory Commission
for the CTBTO and its Provisional Technical Secretariat
in Vienna. Seismic, hydroacoustic, infrasound and radionuclide
data are collected through the stations of the IMS
and transmitted to Member States via the IDC. The IDC
also processes the raw data received from the stations to
derive objective products and services which will support
the Treaty verification responsibilities.
If the collected and analysed data indicate an ambiguous
event, States may address concerns about possible noncompliance

with the Treaty through a consultation and clarification process after it enters into force and may
request an on-site inspection by the CTBTO.

4. History and significance of the CTBT

The Comprehensive Nuclear-Test-Ban Treaty (CTBT) was
negotiated and drafted in the Conference on Disarmament
in Geneva and opened for signature in New York in 1996.

In the first 50 years following the first nuclear weapon test,
there were multiple unsuccessful attempts to negotiate a
comprehensive test ban. The conclusion of the CTBT essentially
ended 50 years of testing, thus achieving one goal of
the States Parties to the 1963 Limited Test-Ban Treaty and

the 1968 Treaty on the Non-Proliferation of Nuclear Weapons (NPT): the discontinuance of all nuclear weapon test explosions for all time. The conclusion of the CTBT was one of the conditions upon which States Parties to the NPT agreed to the indefinite extension of the NPT in 1995. At its 2000 Review Conference, NPT States Parties concluded that signature, ratification and entry into force of the CTBT are "the first practical step for the systematic and progressive efforts to implement article VI of the NPT", with its aim of nuclear disarmament. In that same year, the United Nations Secretary-General included the CTBT as one of the 25 core multilateral treaties representative of the key objectives of the United Nations, prompting many of the States to take action on the CTBT during the Millennium Assembly and thereafter. Prospects for entry into force of the CTBT received a much needed boost in April 2009 when US President Barack Obama announced that his administration will "immediately and aggressively" seek the consent of the US Senate for US ratification. Other Annex 2 States such as China also indicated that they too are eager to achieve entry into force at an early date. The Indonesian Foreign Minister's announcement in April 2010 that his country (another Annex 2 State) will ratify the CTBT soon provided significant additional momentum. The international support for the Treaty is further evidenced through the overwhelming support for the 2009 CTBT resolution at the First Committee of the United Nations General Assembly, the Security Council's call upon States to bring the CTBT into force as expressed in resolution 1887, and the unprecedented high level attendance at the 2009 Conference on Facilitating the Entry into Force of the CTBT. The Final Document of the 2010 NPT Review Conference reaffirmed the vital importance of the entry into force of the CTBT as a core element of the international nuclear disarmament and non-proliferation regime.

5. Membership benefits

Politically, States Signatories contribute to regional and international peace and security, support the NPT and United Nations goals of nuclear non-proliferation and disarmament, and join a community of like-minded States. The 337 CTBTO International Monitoring System facilities currently being built in accordance with the Treaty (170 seismic, 11 hydroacoustic, 60 infrasound and 80 radionuclide stations and 16 radionuclide laboratories) are located all over the world, including some in the most remote regions such as the Arctic and Antarctica. It is multilateralism at its best: 89 countries from North and South, East and West, are hosting or will host the facilities that no country could build and

deploy alone. These countries and the exact location of the
stations are established by Annex 1 to the Protocol to the
Treaty. As one of the most extensive global joint ventures,
hundreds of station operators and National Data Centre staff
support the system around the world around the clock. They
represent a nearly invisible, but highly efficient and crucial
extended arm of the monitoring system.
The raw data as well as processed data products are transmitted,
upon request, to States Signatories by the IDC in Vienna.
The Preparatory Commission can assist States Signatories in
the establishment of National Data Centres by providing the

satellite link to the IDC and assistance with its installation,
software, services of the Help Desk, and specialized training
for station operators and managers. States Signatories
can make use of the range of technologies applied in collecting,
transmitting, processing and analysing verification
related data. They may also benefit from the utilization of
verification regime data in a variety of civil areas, including
scientific research, disaster preparedness, meteorological
and climate forecasting, and tsunami warning. The training
courses and workshops are free of charge and are very important
to building the capacity of States Signatories to make the
best use of the verification related technologies, including for

civil and scientific applications.
As the installation of the IMS progresses, new research
and improved communications technology strengthen and
refine the detection capacities of the system.
Currently, 114 States Signatories have established National
Data Centres to receive and process the data and data products
collected by the IMS and transmitted by the IDC in
Vienna. More than 1145 users worldwide are receiving data
through their State's Secure Signatory Account.

6. N ational implementation measures

6.1. How?

Article III of the CTBT requires each State Party to take, in
accordance with its constitutional processes, any necessary

measures to implement its obligations under the Treaty.

Even in States having a legal system where treaties automatically form part of national law, the government may need to adopt at least some measures, legislative and/or administrative, to implement the Treaty. It is for each State Party to decide what measures, in accordance with its constitutional processes, would be necessary or appropriate and how to carry them out.

In some cases, the State may determine that existing national legislation already fulfils the requirements set out in the Treaty. In most cases, existing legislation may need to be amended or supplemented, or one or more new laws may need to be passed, and subsidiary regulations or administrative measures may need to be adopted. Whatever approaches the State decides to follow, the common goal is to give internal legal effect to all of the State's obligations under the Treaty and, in particular, to enable it to legally enforce those obligations in respect of activities by all persons under its jurisdiction, including by means of sanctions for violations.

6.2. What measures?

Section 8 below provides a checklist of the main elements of national legislation to be considered.

6.3. Where?

The legislation shall apply to the whole territory of the

State and must be extended to any other place under its jurisdiction or control in accordance with international law. Furthermore, Article III requires that the legislation be extended extraterritorially to natural persons possessing the State's nationality, to prohibit such persons from undertaking anywhere any activity prohibited by the Treaty.

6.4. When?

The necessary national implementation measures need to be in force at the time the CTBT enters into force. As a general rule, the measures should therefore be taken either at the time of ratification or immediately afterwards. In many States, the legislature has often stipulated that the legislation will enter into force when the CTBT does. In other cases, the State has

decided to adopt the national normative constraints against
nuclear testing with immediate effect, in advance of the Treaty's
entry into force, as an environmental, counterterrorism
or other policy based measure.
Since 2004, the adoption and enforcement of effective laws
and the establishment of a range of domestic controls aimed
at preventing nuclear weapon proliferation among non-State
actors, in particular for terrorist purposes, have become the
obligation of all States under United Nations Security Council
resolution 1540. The creation of the criminal offence of
carrying out a nuclear explosion, with penalties appropriate
to the gravity of the crime, together with measures aimed at

preventing the acquisition of enabling materials or devices, acts to deter persons from undertaking such activities in the State's jurisdiction and prevent the State's territory from being a haven for those who might be interested in pursuing such activities. Such legislation serves to meet the requirements of resolution 1540, a binding legal obligation for all States under the Charter of the United Nations. For these reasons, a number of States have already made it a criminal offence to carry out a nuclear explosion or to cause, encourage, attempt, assist with or in any way participate in one. Some States, at the time of ratifying the CTBT, amended their penal code with immediate effect. Others had already adopted such legislation as nuclear-weapon-free-zone States. Examples of such types of legislation are available from the CTBTO Secretariat upon request.

Finally, owing to the extensive activities that are required to be taken by the CTBTO Preparatory Commission and States Signatories to establish and provisionally operate the IMS and IDC during the preparatory phase, the State may find that it needs to take measures to enable effective cooperation with the Commission now.

7. The National Authority

Article III of the CTBT requires each State Party to designate or set up a National Authority to "serve as the national focal point for liaison with the Organization and with other States Parties".

The core function of the National Authority is to facilitate the interaction between States and with the CTBTO on all matters regarding the implementation of the Treaty after its entry into force. Before entry into force of the Treaty, most States Signatories have already set up at least an interim National Authority because of the need to cooperate with the Commission in establishing the verification regime. For States hosting monitoring facilities, the National Authority

usually is the governmental entity which negotiates and
promotes the conclusion of the necessary Facility Agreement
in order to advance work on the IMS, which must
be fully operational at entry into force. In other States, the
National Authority is cooperating with the Commission
in establishing a National Data Centre and building the
national capacity to receive and analyse IMS data.

In the event of an on-site inspection after entry into force
of the Treaty, the role of the National Authority would be
particularly important, considering the negotiations and
administrative arrangements required to facilitate inspection
activities under the Treaty. Such tasks would include

communication between the inspected State Party and the
Technical Secretariat, consultations on the mandate of the
inspection, and privileges and immunities, as well as visas,
diplomatic clearance for the inspection aircraft or exemption
issues.

The establishment or designation of the National Authority
is mainly an administrative matter. It would usually be
established as a result of general executive powers of the
government. While it is therefore not necessary to include
it in an implementing act or statute, it may be necessary to
establish its mandate and powers by statute, in particular

when its powers would affect the rights of third parties or
it has been assigned some level of enforcement authority.
Currently, more than 130 States Signatories have designated
their respective National Authorities.

8. Checklist for legislators

The sections below identify elements that are suggested to be
taken into account by States when incorporating the Treaty
into national law. The CTBTO Secretariat has developed and
freely distributes a guide to CTBT legislation which contains
model legislation and commentary. The Secretariat is also
available for consultations or assistance.

8.1. M easures explicitly required

- Prohibit and prevent nuclear weapon test explosions and any other nuclear explosion;

- Extend the legislation extraterritorially to natural
persons possessing the State's nationality regardless
of where the persons commit the act;
- Cooperate with, and afford legal assistance to, other
States Parties;
- Designate or set up a National Authority.

8.2. Other elements normally necessary

- Definitions;
- Law that is binding also on the government;
- Recognition of the legal capacity of the CTBTO;
- Privileges and immunities of the CTBTO, delegates
of its Member States, staff and experts;
- Confidentiality of data;
- For States hosting a facility in the CTBTO International
Monitoring System, national arrangements

to enable site selection, construction, operation,
maintenance and data transmission;
- Procedures to report chemical explosions above the
threshold established by the Treaty;
- Inspection powers and procedures;
- Authority to issue regulations;
- Allocation of budgetary and personnel resources to
participate in the CTBTO and its activities.

8.3. Measures which may be necessary during the
preparatory phase

To establish and provisionally operate the IMS and IDC
during the preparatory phase, some States Signatories have
adopted measures to:
- Establish or designate the National Authority and
National Data Centre;
- Recognize the legal capacity of the Preparatory

Commission;

- Confer privileges and immunities upon the Preparatory Commission, delegates, the Executive Secretary, staff and experts;
- Authorize the negotiation and conclusion of Facility Agreements or Arrangements with the Preparatory Commission;
- Authorize and enable the conduct of activities pursuant to the Resolution establishing the Preparatory Commission, including cooperation between the National Authority and the Preparatory Commission;
- Allocate budgetary and personnel resources to participate in the Commission and its activities.

9. Ratifying States (153 as of May 2010)

Afghanistan, Albania, Algeria*, Andorra, Antigua and
Barbuda, Argentina*, Armenia, Australia*, Austria*,
Azerbaijan, Bahamas, Bahrain, Bangladesh*, Barbados,
Belarus, Belgium*, Belize, Benin, Bolivia (Plurinational
State of), Bosnia and Herzegovina, Botswana, Brazil*,
Bulgaria*, Burkina Faso, Burundi, Cambodia, Cameroon,
Canada*, Cape Verde, Central African Republic, Chile*,
Colombia*, Cook Islands, Costa Rica, Côte d'Ivoire, Croatia,
Cyprus, Czech Republic, Democratic Republic of the
Congo*, Denmark, Djibouti, Dominican Republic, Ecuador,
El Salvador, Eritrea, Estonia, Ethiopia, Fiji, Finland*,
France*, Gabon, Georgia, Germany*, Greece, Grenada,

Guyana, Haiti, Holy See, Honduras, Hungary*, Iceland,
Ireland, Italy*, Jamaica, Japan*, Jordan, Kazakhstan, Kenya,
Kiribati, Kuwait, Kyrgyzstan, Lao People's Democratic
Republic, Latvia, Lebanon, Lesotho, Liberia, Libyan
Arab Jamahiriya, Liechtenstein, Lithuania, Luxembourg,

Madagascar, Malawi, Malaysia, Maldives, Mali, Malta,
Marshall Islands, Mauritania, Mexico*, Micronesia
(Federated States of), Monaco, Mongolia, Montenegro,
Morocco, Mozambique, Namibia, Nauru, Netherlands*,
New Zealand, Nicaragua, Niger, Nigeria, Norway*, Oman,

Palau, Panama, Paraguay, Peru*, Philippines, Poland*,
Portugal, Qatar, Republic of Korea*, Republic of Moldova,
Romania*, Russian Federation*, Rwanda, Saint Kitts and
Nevis, Saint Lucia, Saint Vincent and the Grenadines, Samoa,
San Marino, Senegal, Serbia, Seychelles, Sierra Leone,
Singapore, Slovakia*, Slovenia, South Africa*, Spain*,
Sudan, Suriname, Sweden*, Switzerland*, Tajikistan, The
former Yugoslav Republic of Macedonia, Togo, Trinidad
and Tobago, Tunisia, Turkey*, Turkmenistan, Uganda,
Ukraine*, United Arab Emirates, United Kingdom of Great
Britain and Northern Ireland*, United Republic of Tanzania,
Uruguay, Uzbekistan, Vanuatu, Venezuela (Bolivarian

Republic of), Viet Nam* and Zambia.

10. Signatory States which have not yet ratified (29 as of May 2010)

Angola, Brunei Darussalam, Chad, China*, Comoros, Congo, Egypt*, Equatorial Guinea, Gambia, Ghana, Guatemala, Guinea, Guinea-Bissau, Indonesia*, Iran (Islamic Republic of)*, Iraq, Israel*, Myanmar, Nepal, Papua New Guinea, Sao Tome and Principe, Solomon Islands, Sri Lanka, Swaziland, Thailand, Timor-Leste, United States of America*, Yemen and Zimbabwe.

* States, listed in Annex 2, which must ratify the CTBT before it can enter into force.

11. Non-signatory States

(13 as of May 2010)
Bhutan, Cuba, Democratic People's Republic of Korea*,
Dominica, India*, Mauritius, Niue, Pakistan*, Saudi Arabia,
Somalia, Syrian Arab Republic, Tonga and Tuvalu.

12. Entry into force

The CTBT will enter into force 180 days after it has been
ratified by the 44 States listed in Annex 2. These 44 States
formally participated in the negotiations of the Treaty and
possessed nuclear power reactors or research reactors at the
time. Nine of those States have not yet ratified the Treaty.

13. Resolutions by the Inter-Parliamentary Union

13.1. Resolutions 1995–2009

The Inter-Parliamentary Union has adopted a series of resolutions

in which either explicit reference is made to the CTBT
or the stated aims are consistent with those of the CTBT:

- The Importance of Adhering to the Obligations
Specified in the Treaty on the Non-Proliferation of
Nuclear Weapons (91st Inter-Parliamentary Conference/
Paris, 1994)

* States, listed in Annex 2, which must ratify the CTBT before it can
enter into force.

- To Comprehensively Ban Nuclear Weapons Testing
and Halt All Present Nuclear Weapons Tests (94th
Inter-Parliamentary Conference/Bucharest, 1995)

- Parliamentary Action to Encourage all Countries
to Sign and Ratify the Comprehensive Test Ban
Treaty Prohibiting All Nuclear Testing, to Encourage
Universal and Non-discriminatory Nuclear Non-Proliferation Measures and to Work Towards the
Eventual Elimination of All Nuclear Weapons (101st
Inter-Parliamentary Conference/Brussels, 1999)
- Importance of the Non-Proliferation of Nuclear,
Chemical and Biological Weapons of Mass Destruction
and of Missiles, Including the Prevention of
their Use by Terrorists (108th Inter-Parliamentary
Conference/Santiago (Chile), 2003)
- The Role of Parliaments in Assisting Multilateral
Organisations in Ensuring Peace and Security and
in Building an International Coalition for Peace

(109th IPU Assembly/Geneva, 2003)
- The Announcement by the Democratic People's
Republic of Korea of its Nuclear Weapons Test and
the Strengthening of the Nuclear Non-Proliferation
Regime (115th IPU Assembly/Geneva, 2006)
- Advancing Nuclear Non-Proliferation and Disarmament,
and Securing the Entry into Force of the
Comprehensive Nuclear-Test-Ban Treaty: the Role
of Parliaments (120th IPU Assembly/Addis Ababa,
2009).

Background Information for Parliamentarians on THE CTBT

20

13.2. Text of the 2009 Resolution

Advancing Nuclear Non-Proliferation and Disarmament,
and Securing the Entry into Force of the

Comprehensive Nuclear-Test-Ban Treaty: the Role of Parliaments

Resolution adopted by consensus* by the 120th IPU Assembly (Addis Ababa, 10 April 2009)

The 120th Assembly of the Inter-Parliamentary Union,

Determined to advance nuclear disarmament and nonproliferation with a view to strengthening international peace and security in accordance with the principles of the Charter of the United Nations, and *underscoring* that substantial progress in the field of nuclear disarmament requires active support and dedicated contributions by all States,

Deeply concerned that the existence in the world of some 26,000 nuclear weapons, whose use can have

devastating human, environmental and economic consequences,
constitutes a threat to international peace and security,

Reaffirming the obligations of nuclear-weapon States
under Article VI of the Treaty on the Non-Proliferation
of Nuclear Weapons (NPT) towards nuclear disarmament
and their unequivocal undertakings under the 1995 and 2000 NPT Review Conferences in this regard,

Recalling past IPU resolutions designed to advance the
progress of non-proliferation and disarmament and to
encourage ratification of the Comprehensive Nuclear-Test-Ban Treaty (CTBT), in particular the one adopted

by the 101st Inter-Parliamentary Conference (Brussels,
April 1999),

Reaffirming the crucial importance of the NPT as the
cornerstone of the nuclear non-proliferation and disarmament
regime, which sets out legal obligations in these fields at the same time as it guarantees the right to
develop nuclear energy for peaceful purposes,

Recalling international conventions and resolutions
adopted by the UN Security Council and the IPU on
the right to access nuclear technology for peaceful
purposes,

Concerned that non-compliance with all provisions of
the NPT by some States has undermined the three pillars
of the NPT and eroded the benefits derived by all

States,

Considering the importance of all States ensuring strict compliance with their nuclear non-proliferation and disarmament obligations,

Recognizing the progress made under the NPT and the resulting safeguards agreements, and *urging* the nuclearweapon States to fully implement the commitments they undertook during the NPT Review Conferences in 1995 and 2000,

Concerned that, in spite of tireless efforts made by the international community for forty years to ban nuclear explosions in all environments, and thirteen years after

it was opened for signature, the CTBT has yet to enter
into force,
Convinced that the verified cessation of nuclearweapon-
test explosions or any other nuclear explosions constitutes an effective disarmament and non-proliferation
measure and is a meaningful preliminary step towards nuclear disarmament, but *stressing* that the
only way to remove the threat of nuclear weapons is
the total elimination of such inhumane weapons,
Stressing that a universal and effectively verifiable
CTBT constitutes a fundamental instrument in the field
of nuclear disarmament and non-proliferation,
Underscoring the crucial role of the International
Atomic Energy Agency (IAEA) in promoting nuclear

cooperation, the transfer of nuclear technology for
peaceful purposes to developing countries, and nuclear
non-proliferation, and the need for every State to adopt
the non-proliferation safeguards standard of a comprehensive
safeguards agreement combined with an additional protocol,

Disappointed that after over a decade, the Conference
on Disarmament, the UN multilateral disarmament
negotiation body, has yet to agree on a programme of
work and resume its important mandate, owing to the
divergent views on disarmament negotiation priorities,

Considering the important role played by bilateral
disarmament treaties, such as the Strategic Arms
Reduction Treaty, *welcoming* the cuts made by some
nuclear-weapon States to their nuclear arsenals and
urging deeper, faster and irreversible cuts to all types
of nuclear weapons by all nuclear-armed States,

Convinced that the best way to guarantee world peace
and stability is to take effective measures for international
security, including disarmament and the non-proliferation of nuclear weapons,

Recognizing the benefits of confidence-building measures,
such as the de-emphasizing of nuclear weapons
in national security doctrines and the removal of
nuclear weapons systems from high alert status, and

mindful of the mutual confidence engendered by freely
agreed regional nuclear-weapon-free zones, such as
those in the South Pacific, Africa, South-East Asia and
Latin America,

Underscoring the importance of establishing a
nuclear-weapon-free zone in the Middle East, without
exception,

Deeply concerned by the risk of accidental or unauthorized
use of nuclear weapons and by the resulting toll in
human life, environmental damage, political tensions,
economic loss and market instability,

Pledging to bring about fuller parliamentary involvement
in the disarmament process, particularly in respect

of nuclear weapons, in the form of greater pressure on
governments and detailed scrutiny of military budgets
and procurement programmes allocated for nuclear
weapons development,

Mindful of the fact that national defence policies
should not compromise the fundamental principle of
undiminished security for all, and thus *recalling* that
any unilateral deployment or build-up of strategic antiballistic
missile assets affecting the deterrent capacity of
nuclear-weapon States might hinder the process of
nuclear disarmament,

1. *Calls on* all nuclear-armed States to make deeper,
faster and irreversible cuts to all types of nuclear

weapons;
2. *Urges* all States to redouble their efforts to prevent
and combat the proliferation of nuclear and other
weapons of mass destruction in accordance with
international law;
3. *Underscores* the vital role of the CTBT as part of a
framework for achieving nuclear non-proliferation
and disarmament, and *expresses disappointment*
that, thirteen years after it was opened for signature,
the Treaty has yet to enter into force;
4. *Stresses* the vital importance and urgency of signature
and ratification, without delay and without conditions, to achieve the earliest entry into force
of the CTBT;

5. *Welcomes* the signatures/ratifications of the CTBT
in 2008 by Barbados, Burundi, Colombia, Lebanon,
Malawi, Malaysia, Mozambique and Timor-Leste;

6. *Calls upon* the parliaments of all States that have
not yet signed and ratified the CTBT to exert pressure
on their governments to do so;

7. *Especially urges* parliaments of all remaining States listed in Annex 2 of the CTBT, whose ratification
is required to bring the treaty into force, to urge their governments to immediately sign and ratify
the treaty;

8. *Calls on* all nuclear-armed States to continue to

observe their moratoria on nuclear-weapon testing,
on all States that have not already done so to proceed, on a voluntary basis, to dismantle their
nuclear test sites, and on all States to maintain support
for the CTBT Organization verification system until the CTBT enters into force;

9. *Urges* immediate commencement of negotiations
on a non-discriminatory, multilateral and internationally
verifiable treaty banning the production of fissile material for nuclear weapons and other
nuclear explosive devices;

10. *Invites* States to initiate negotiations with a view
to concluding a treaty on the prohibition of shortrange
and intermediate-range land missiles that carry nuclear warheads;

11. *Recommends* that States with ballistic missile capacity that have not acceded to the Hague Code of Conduct do so quickly in order to render this instrument completely effective against ballistic missile proliferation;

12. *Calls* on all nuclear-armed States to adopt confidencebuilding measures, including the de-emphasizing of nuclear weapons in national security doctrines and the removal of all nuclear weapons from high alert status;

13. *Reaffirms* the importance of achieving universal accession to the NPT, and of States not party to the NPT acceding to it promptly and unconditionally as non-nuclear-weapon States, and of all States

party to the NPT fulfilling their obligations under
the Treaty;

14. *Is hopeful* that the States concerned will be required
to sign and comply with safeguards agreements and
additional protocols, in particular those concluded
in the framework of the IAEA, as a prerequisite for
benefiting from international cooperation in the field of nuclear energy for civilian purposes;

15. *Calls on* all States to support the initiatives aimed
at globalizing the obligations set forth in the Treaty
signed between the United States and the former
Soviet Union on the elimination of their intermediate-
range and shorter-range missiles (INF Treaty) and to promote cooperative approaches to the issue

of missile defence, beginning with a joint assessment
of possible threats;

16. *Calls on* national parliaments to ensure State compliance
with all their disarmament and non-proliferation
obligations;

17. *Urges* parliaments to provide strong and effective
support to all resolutions and recommendations
on peace, disarmament and security previously
adopted at IPU Conferences and Assemblies;

18. *Encourages* parliaments to monitor closely national
implementation of all arms control, non-proliferation
and disarmament treaties and UN resolutions,
to engage their publics on nuclear issues and to
report back to the IPU on progress made;

19. *Urges* IAEA Member States or parties to a safeguards
agreement to lend strong and constant support to the IAEA so that it can honour its safeguards obligations and therefore to cooperate in good faith
with the IAEA by providing it with all information
requested;

20. *Calls on* States whose ratification is needed for the
entry into force of general safeguards agreements
to take the necessary steps to that end as soon as
possible;

21. *Further calls on* the States party to a safeguards
agreement which have not yet signed and/or ratified
an additional protocol to do so as soon as possible;

22. *Recommends* that the United Nations, especially

the Office of Disarmament Affairs, and the Preparatory Commission for the CTBT Organization, strengthen cooperation with the IPU;

23. *Invites* the IPU Secretary General to contact, on an annual basis, the parliaments of the States which have not signed and/or ratified the international treaties mentioned in the present resolution with a view to encouraging them to do so;

24. *Urges* parliaments to instruct governments to express their support for the UN Secretary-General's Five Point Proposal contained in his address, "The United Nations and Security in a Nuclear-Weapon-Free World";

25. *Encourages* parliaments to support the full ratification

and implementation of existing nuclear-weapon-free zones, and to explore the possibility of establishing additional nuclear-weapon-free zones freely agreed by States in specific regions;

26. *Calls for* the necessary steps to be taken to declare the Middle East a nuclear-weapon-free zone, without exception, in keeping with the resolution endorsed by the NPT Review Conference in 1995;

27. *Encourages* all parliaments to remain seized of the issue at the highest political level and, where possible, to promote compliance with the NPT through bilateral and joint outreach, seminars and other means.

* The following delegations expressed reservations on parts of the resolution:
- China — operative paragraphs 10, 11 and 15;
- India — preambular paragraphs 4, 5, 7, 10 and 12 and operative paragraphs 3, 4, 6, 7, 8 and 13;
- Iran (Islamic Republic of) — preambular paragraph 18 and operative paragraphs 6, 10, 21 and 26;
- Pakistan — preambular paragraphs 7 and 13 and operative paragraphs 13, 14, 16, 17, 18 and 23.

Chapter -2

Dirty Bomb

A **radiological attack** is the spreading of radioactive material with the intent to do harm. Radioactive materials are used every day in laboratories, medical centers, food irradiation plants, and for industrial uses. If stolen or otherwise acquired, many of these materials could be used in a "radiological dispersal device" (RDD).

Radiological Dispersal Devices, a.k.a. Dirty Bombs

A **"dirty bomb"** is one type of RDD that uses a conventional explosion to disperse radioactive material over a targeted area. The term dirty bomb and RDD are often used interchangeably in technical literature. However, RDDs could also include other means of dispersal such as placing a container of radioactive material in a public place, or using an airplane to disperse powdered or aerosolized forms of radioactive material.

A Dirty Bomb Is Not a Nuclear Bomb

A nuclear bomb creates an explosion that is thousands to millions of times more powerful than any conventional explosive that might be used in a dirty bomb. The resulting mushroom cloud from a nuclear detonation contains fine particles of radioactive dust and other debris that can blanket large areas (tens to hundreds of square miles) with "fallout." By contrast, most of the radioactive particles dispersed by a dirty bomb would likely fall to the ground within a few city blocks or miles of the explosion.

How an RDD Might be Used
It is very difficult to design an RDD that would deliver radiation doses high enough to cause immediate health effects or fatalities in a large number of people. Therefore, experts generally agree that an RDD would most likely be used to:

Contaminate facilities or places where people live and work, disrupting lives and livelihoods. Cause anxiety in those who think they are being, or have been, exposed.

Detection and Measurement
Radiation can be readily detected with equipment carried by many emergency responders, such as Geiger counters, which provide a measure of radiation dose rate. Other

types of instruments are used to identify the radioactive element(s) present.

> "The ease of recovery from [a radiological] attack would depend to a great extent on how the attack was handled by first responders, political leaders, and the news media, all of which would help to shape public opinion and reactions."
>
> **Making the Nation Safer**
> National Research Council (2002)

What is ionizing radiation?

When radioactive elements decay, they produce energetic emissions (alpha particles, beta particles, or gamma rays) that can cause chemical changes in tissues. The average person in the United States receives a "background" dose of about one-third of a rem* per year—about 80% from natural sources including earth materials and cosmic radiation, and the remaining 20% from man-made radiation sources, such as medical x-rays. There are different types of radioactive materials that emit different kinds of radiation:

Gamma and X-rays can travel long distances in air and can pass through the body exposing internal organs; it is also a concern if gamma emitting material is ingested or inhaled.

Beta radiation can travel a few yards in the air and in sufficient quantities might cause skin damage; beta-emitting material is an internal hazard if ingested or inhaled.

Alpha radiation travels only an inch or two in the air and cannot even penetrate skin; alpha-emitting material is a hazard if it is ingested or inhaled.

* A rem is a measure of radiation dose, based on the amount of energy absorbed in a mass of tissue. Dose can also be measured in Sieverts (1 Sievert=100 rem

WHAT DO RDDS DO?

The Area Affected

Most dirty bombs and other RDDs would have very localized effects, ranging from less than a city block to several square miles. The area over which radioactive materials would be dispersed depends on factors such as:

- Amount and type of radioactive material dispersed. • Means of dispersal (e.g. explosion, spraying, fire). • Physical and chemical form of the radioactive material. For example, if the material is dispersed as fine particles, it might be carried by the wind over a relatively large area. • Local topography, location of buildings, and other landscape characteristics. • Local weather conditions.

Spread of a Radioactive Plume

If the radioactive material is release as fine particles, the plume would spread roughly with the speed and direction of the wind. As a radioactive plume spreads over a larger area, the radioactivity becomes less concentrated. Atmospheric models might be used to estimate the location and movement of a radioactive plume.

WHAT IS THE DANGER?

Immediate Impact to Human Health

Most injuries from a dirty bomb would probably occur from the heat, debris, radiological dust, and force of the conventional explosion used to disperse the radioactive material, affecting only individuals close to the site of the explosion. At the low radiation levels expected from an RDD, the immediate health effects from radiation exposure would likely be minimal.

Health Effects of Radiation Exposure

Health effects of radiation exposure are determined by the:

- Amount of radiation absorbed by the body.
- Radiation type (see "What is ionizing radiation?," p.1).
- Means of exposure—external or internal (absorbed by the skin, inhaled, or ingested).
- Length of time exposed.

The health effects of radiation tend to be directly proportional to radiation dose. If a reasonable estimate can be made of a person's dose, a lot is known about the health effects at that dose.

Acute Radiation Syndrome (ARS)

ARS is not likely to result from a dirty bomb. It is a short-term health effect that begins to appear when individuals are exposed to a highly radioactive material over a relatively small amount of time. The chart shows that an estimated 10% of the population may exhibit signs of ARS if they are exposed to large radiation doses of 100 rems or more. Principal signs and symptoms of ARS are nausea, vomiting, diarrhea, and reduced blood cell counts.

Psychological Impacts

Psychological effects from fear of being exposed may be one of the major consequences of a dirty bomb. Unless information about potential exposure is made available from a credible source, people unsure about their exposure might seek advice from medical cent

Are Terrorists Interested In Radioactive Materials?

Yes, terrorists have been interested in acquiring radioactive and nuclear material for use in attacks. For example, in 1995, Chechen extremists threatened to bundle radioactive material with explosives to use against Russia in order to force the Russian military to withdraw from Chechnya. While no explosives were used, officials later retrieved a package of cesium-137 the rebels had buried in a Moscow park.

Since September 11, 2001, terrorist arrests and prosecutions overseas have revealed that individuals associated with al-Qaeda planned to acquire materials for a RDD. In 2004, British authorities arrested a British national, Dhiren Barot, and several associates on various charges, including conspiring to commit public nuisance by the use of radioactive materials. In 2006, Barot was found guilty and sentenced to life. British authorities disclosed that Barot developed a document known as the "Final Presentation." The document outlined his research on the production of "dirty bombs," which he characterized as designed to "cause injury, fear, terror and chaos" rather than to kill. U.S. federal prosecutors indicted Barot and two associates for conspiracy to use weapons of mass destruction against persons within the United States, in conjunction with the alleged surveillance of several

landmarks and office complexes in Washington, D.C., New York City, and Newark, N.J. In a separate
British police operation in 2004, authorities arrested British national, Salahuddin Amin, and six others on terrorism-related charges. Amin is accused of making inquiries about buying a "radioisotope bomb" from the Russian mafia in Belgium; and the group is alleged to have linkages to al-Qaeda. Nothing appeared to have come from his inquiries, according to British prosecutors. While neither Barot nor Amin had the opportunity to carry their plans forward to an operational stage, these arrests demonstrate the continued interest of terrorists in acquiring and using radioactive material for malicious purposes.

Will

Chapter - 3

Nuclear Testing

The more than 2,000 nuclear tests that have been conducted worldwide
by the nuclear powers since 1945 have not been without consequences.
Many areas that served as test sites continue to suffer from the horrific
health and environmental effects of nuclear explosions. For example, in
the Semipalatinsk region in Eastern Kazakhstan, which served as the

prime test site for Soviet nuclear testing, the average life expectancy is
less than 50 years, the death rate is extremely high, and cancer rates have
reached critical levels. Moreover, serious birth defects are common, with
incidences of mental retardation three to five times higher than average.
Some of the nuclear-weapon States have introduced compensation
schemes for victims of their nuclear tests

While the CTBT was opened for signature in 1996,5 it has not entered into force, leaving a ban on
nuclear testing as the oldest item on the arms control agenda. Efforts to curtail tests have been
made since the 1940s. In the 1950s, the United States and Soviet Union conducted hundreds of hydrogen bomb tests. The radioactive fallout from these tests spurred worldwide protest. These

pressures, plus a desire to improve U.S.-Soviet relations in the wake of the Cuban Missile Crisis of 1962, led to the Limited Test Ban Treaty of 1963, which banned nuclear explosions in the atmosphere, in space, and under water. The Threshold Test Ban Treaty, signed in 1974, banned
underground nuclear weapons tests having an explosive force of more than 150 kilotons, the equivalent of 150,000 tons of TNT, 10 times the force of the Hiroshima bomb. The Peaceful Nuclear Explosions Treaty, signed in 1976, extended the 150-kiloton limit to nuclear explosions
for peaceful purposes. President Carter did not pursue ratification of these treaties, preferring to
negotiate a comprehensive test ban treaty, or CTBT, a ban on all nuclear explosions. When agreement on a CTBT seemed near, however, he pulled back, bowing to arguments that continued

testing was needed to maintain reliability of existing weapons, to develop new weapons, and for other purposes. President Reagan raised concerns about U.S. ability to monitor the two unratified treaties and late in his term started negotiations on new verification protocols. These two treaties were ratified in 1990.

With the end of the Cold War, the need for improved warheads dropped and pressures for a CTBT grew. The U.S.S.R. and France began nuclear test moratoria in October 1990 and April 1992, respectively. In early 1992, many in Congress favored a one-year test moratorium. The effort led to the Hatfield-Exon-Mitchell amendment to the FY1993 Energy and Water Development Appropriations Bill, which banned testing before July 1, 1993, set conditions on a resumption of

testing, banned testing after September 1996 unless another nation tested, and required the President to report to Congress annually on a plan to achieve a CTBT by September 30, 1996. President George H. W. Bush signed the bill into law (P.L. 102-377) October 2, 1992. The CTBT was negotiated in the Conference on Disarmament. It was adopted by the U.N. General Assembly
on September 10, 1996, and was opened for signature on September 24, 1996. As of June 2013,
183 states had signed it and 159 had ratified.6

Table 2. U.S. Nuclear Tests by Calendar Year

1945-1949	6	1960-1964	202	1980-1984	92
1950-1954	43	1965-1969	231	1985-1989	75
1955-1959	145	1970-1974	137	1990-1992	23
1975-1979	100	Total	1054		

Source: U.S. Department of Energy

Arms Control Association
Section 3

information from the IMS and disseminates the raw and processed data to member states for their own evaluation.

The nuclear-weapon states are well monitored, with 32 IMS sites in Russia, 12 in China and 39 in the United States. The South American cone has 23 sites in Argentina, Brazil, and Chile. North Korea is well covered with 23 sites in China, Japan, and South Korea. The Middle East has 17 sites. India and Pakistan are surrounded with more than 40 sites in Australia, Bangladesh, China, Sri Lanka, and Thailand.

To these assets must be added the IMS sites not listed here, hundreds of seismographs that are not part of the IMS, and additional data from U.S. intelligence services.36

Importantly, the CTBT recognizes the right of the United States and others to monitor compliance using their own highly sophisticated satellites and other national technical means (NTM). In the United States, the Air Force Technical Applications Center (AFTAC) operates a global network of nuclear event detection sensors called the U.S. Atomic Energy Detection System (USAEDS). This system can detect a suspicious event underground, underwater, in the atmosphere and in space. In addition to the CTBT, AFTAC

If CTBT parties know the treaty is effectively verifiable, cheating would be deterred because the

potential gains of a nuclear test that might escape
detection would be small (not militarily significant)
and the potential costs would be high in terms of
international reaction and the possibility of sanctions
and military measures in response. The goal of the
CTBT verification system is thus not only to detect
significant cheating, but to *deter violations in the first
place* by convincing potential cheaters that the risks
and costs of cheating outweigh any plausible benefits.

Global Alarm System

The CTBT established the International Monitoring
System (IMS) to detect potential nuclear explosions
using four primary technologies: seismic,

hydroacoustic, radionuclide, and infrasound. Since 1999, 160 additional IMS stations have been built and, of the planned 337 IMS facilities, to date 276 have been built and 28 are under construction. New technologies such as InSAR (Interferometric Synthetic Aperture Radar) can now pinpoint the location of an explosion within 100 meters. An International Data Center based in Vienna collects and analyzes

The Comprehensive Test Ban Treaty Is Effectively Verifiable

As of now, the [Comprehensive Test Ban Treaty Organization] is capable of performing the monitoring

mission given to it by the Treaty. And as of tomorrow, no State will be able to carry out a nuclear test
without the knowledge of the international community.

—**Bernard Kouchner**, Foreign Minister of France, September 2009

The goal for any treaty monitoring regime is to provide effective verification. It is generally recognized that no verification system gives absolute assurances. Effective verification means that any attempts to cheat in ways that could threaten U.S. national security must be uncovered in a timely manner. Describing this concept in the context of the Intermediate Nuclear Forces Treaty, Ambassador Paul Nitze said, "If the other side moves beyond the limits of the treaty in any militarily significant way, we would be able to detect such violation in time to respond effectively and thereby deny the other side the benefit of the violation."35

Now More Than Ever

monitors compliance with the 1963 Limited Test Ban Treaty, the 1974 Threshold Test Ban Treaty, and the 1976 Peaceful Nuclear Explosions Treaty.37 In the event of a suspected nuclear explosion that cannot be resolved by remote sensing, once the CTBT is in force states may call for shortnotice, on-site inspections (OSIs) of a suspected test location. The Preparatory Commission for the Comprehensive Test Ban Treaty Organization (CTBTO) in Vienna has been conducting field exercises to test different on-site inspection methods. In September 2008, it carried out a simulated on-site inspection at the former Soviet nuclear test site at Semipalatinsk, Kazakhstan, which demonstrated that

the organization has the capacity to conduct a real
OSI once the treaty is enacted. On-site inspection
requests can be based on IMS data or solely on a
state's national intelligence data. According

The materials removed to create a test shaft and
cavity must be hidden from satellites.
3) Crater and surface changes due to testing must be
hidden from space-based InSAR, a remote sensing
technique that uses radar satellite images and
other technologies. The Indian, North Korean, and
Pakistani test sites were located with commercial
satellite images.

4) Practically all the radioactive gases and particles
must be trapped. Detectors on airplanes can fly into radionuclide plumes.

5) Cheaters must avoid detection of weak seismic
signals by closer stations and arrays; and

6) Cheaters must prevent detection by NTM, which
are more powerful than the IMS at specific locations. Human intelligence must also be considered; it provided the locations of Iran's enrichment facilities and other clandestine sites. 42

As for potential mine masking scenarios, where mining explosions would be used to "hide" a nuclear
one, most chemical explosions in mines are ripplefired
and thus distinct from single-point nuclear explosions. A high-yield, singled-fired mine explosion

is rare and would draw suspicion and inspection.
Again, the need for multiple tests would increase the risk. The NAS study concluded that "taking all factors into account and assuming a fully functional IMS, we judge that an underground nuclear explosion cannot be confidently hidden if its yield is larger than 1 or 2 [kilotons]."43

What Is Militarily Significant?

Ultimately, the United States must be confident that no nation could alter the strategic balance between it and the United States through successful cheating under the CTBT. The NAS study concluded that it would be very difficult for states with less nuclear testing experience, such as India, Iran, North Korea, and Pakistan, to conduct small tests in secret because controlling yields of less than 1 kiloton is technically challenging. Moreover, the information that could be gained from tests in this yield range would have limited use for states that already have simple fission weapons. The NAS also found that states with extensive testing experience (China and Russia) would be more likely to succeed at clandestine testing but do not have the technical need to try, nor would such tests significantly alter the military threat they already pose.

In essence, the NAS study concluded that states that might benefit from cheating do not have the

experience to pull it off, and states that could do so
do not need to cheat. Moreover, nuclear explosions
large enough to be useful for advanced weapons
design would likely be detected by the IMS, while
smaller tests that might escape detection would be
much less useful.

For example, the 1995 JASON study concluded that, for the United States, arsenal tests with yields
less than 500 tons are less important than the SSP
for maintaining warheads, and tests at any yield less
than that required to initiate boosting, including hydronuclear (the equivalent of four pounds of TNT
or less) and 100-ton tests, are of limited value.[44]

When it considered ratification of START in 1994,
the U.S. Senate concluded that potential violations
were not militarily significant, meaning that Russia
would gain little from cheating that would alter the
U.S.-Russian strategic balance. By this same standard,
the Senate should find the CTBT effectively verifiable
as well.

New Since 1999

- **In 1999, only 25 percent of the planned International Monitoring System (IMS) facilities had been built. As of 2010, 90 percent of the planned global verification network was completed or under construction.**
- **National technical means (NTM) of verification have improved since 1999 and have greater**

capacity to detect and locate nuclear tests at sensitive locations than the IMS.

- During the Senate debate in 1999, some critics claimed that verification could only detect underground explosions at or above one kiloton in yield. In reality, nuclear test monitoring capabilities were much better than that in 1999 and have improved substantially in the last decade. North Korea's nuclear tests in 2006 and 2009 demonstrated that the CTBT monitoring system is working well and can detect tests well below one kiloton.
- The Global Seismic Network, a public partnership of seism

Chapter - 4

Nuclear Detterence

The main object of punishment is to make commission of an offence an ill bargain for the offender and deter others from committing the crimes. Salmond has said "Punishment is before all thins deterrent and chief aim of law of crimes is to make the evil doer an example and a warning to all that are like minded with him".

He said that offences are committed by reason of a conflict of interests of the offender and the society. Punishment prevents the offences by destroying the conflict of interests by making acts which are injurious to othersas injurious to the doer himself. The end of justice is achieved by inflicting severe punishment on the offenders. THe rigours of detterent punishment acts as a sufficient warning to offenders and also to others but it invariably fails in case of hardened criminals. It is a well known fact that that quite a large number of hardened criminals return to prison soon after their release. They get used to priison life and loose interest in normal life in society.

Nuclear deterrence is persuading an enemy not to attack by making the negative consequences of such an attack much greater than any potential benifits.

The destructive power of nuclear weapons cannot be contained in either space or time. The nuclear weapons has given the mutually assured destruction which is the capacity of two states to destroy each others countries.

According to US President Ronald Reagan he was faced with the prospect of having onlysix minutes, to decide how to respond to a blip on a radar scope and decide whether to release nuclear missiles. How could anyone apply reason at a time like that.

It is well known that thousands of nuclear missiles are ready to fire within minutes under launch on warning policies, putting the US and Russian presidents into the same six minutes to decide on nuclear missiles. The warning times in some other nuclear armed states such as India and Pakistan are even shorter, resembling to non existent.

For the last 65 years, the world has become so used to nuclear weapons that the very thought of people talking about a world free of nuclear weapons was considered idealistic and unsettling, especially for those who have been hard proponents of nuclear theology. After the four former United States' iconic figures of the Cold War – senior statesmen George Shultz, William Perry, Henry Kissinger and Sam Nunn – wrote their first op-ed in the Wall Street Journal in January 2007, a movement for the elimination of nuclear weapons seems to be gradually gaining momentum.

Danger of a catastrophic nuclear explosion

There is a growing realization that two main threats loom large over the horizon that could completely destroy humanity. One is climate change, affected by the world's heavy reliance on hydro-carbon fuels. The other is an even greater danger, posed by a catastrophic nuclear exchange either by design or accident.

The Nuclear Non-Proliferation Treaty (NPT) Review Conference in May 2010 provided a valuable opportunity to draw attention to the serious risks inherent with nuclear weapons and the urgent need to work collectively towards eliminating them. A world free of nuclear weapons was clearly articulated as a goal for the first time in the Conference and the final document, albeit modest, laid a framework for adopting a more comprehensive approach towards this objective.

united states and russia commit to nuclearweapon-free world

In a historic joint statement in April 2009, U.S. President Obama and Russian President Medvedev committed their countries to achieving a nuclear-weapon-free world and subsequently made a modest beginning by signing the new Strategic Arms Reduction Treaty (START). Following the lead of the nuclear super powers, in September 2009 the United Nations Security Council unanimously adopted a resolution calling for the elimination of nuclear weapons.

The primary reason for this change

To substitute preventive war for deterrence is to ignore the fact that traditional nuclear deterrence was directed at states *already armed with nuclear weapons* and was aimed at deterring their *use* in time of crisis or war; it was not enlisted as a means deterring the *acquisition* of nuclear weapons. That task was, at least until 9/11, left primarily to the regime established by the 1968 Treaty on the Non-Proliferation of Nuclear Weapons, also known as the Nuclear Nonproliferation Treaty (NPT), and to the U.S. policy of providing nuclear guarantees to allies that might otherwise have felt the need to develop their own nuclear weapons.

The administration's security strategy is further challenged by the broader question of whether it is possible over the long run to prevent
proliferation of WMD on the part of states determined to acquire them. Traditional nonproliferation
policy implied that nuclear proliferation could be contained and treated all proliferation as undesirable despite evidence that it could be stabilizing as well as destabilizing.3

Moreover, as the American experience with Iraq has shown, preventive war is a costly and risky enterprise subject to the law of unintended consequences. And it is not at all self-evident that preventive war is necessary, at least against states (as opposed to nonstate entities); on the contrary, preventive war may actually encourage proliferation, although the impact of Operation Iraqi Freedom on North Korean and Iranian attitudes toward nuclear weapons remains as yet unclear. In the final analysis, it is not the mere presence of WMD in hostile hands—but rather their use—that kills and destroys. Accordingly, if their use can be deterred—and the evidence suggests that deterrence does work against rogue states if not terrorist organizations, then deterrence of their use is manifestly a much more attractive policy option than war to prevent their acquisition. That is not to deny the inherent difficulty

of maintaining credible deterrence, especially against adversaries whose culture and values are alien to our own. Deterrence is a psychological
phenomenon, and as such is inherently unstable. Nor can one ignore the impossibility of proving the negative. The success of deterrence is measured by events that do not happen, and one cannot demonstrate
conclusively that an enemy refrained from this or that action because of the implicit or explicit threat of unacceptable retaliation. The argument here is that deterrence
should continue to be the policy of first resort in dealing with hostile states acquiring or seeking to acquire WMD and that preventive war—as opposed to preemptive military action aimed at disrupting an imminent attack—is almost always a bad and ultimately self-defeating option. Richard K. Betts at Columbia University observes that past American arguments

se would have been taken, because of the belief or strong suspicion that intolerable consequences would ensue from such action."7

With respect to nuclear deterrence, nuclear strategist Albert Wohlstetter, in his seminal January 1959 *Foreign Affairs* article, "The Delicate Balance of Terror," put it in a nutshell: "To deter an attack means being able to strike back in spite of it. It means, in other words, a capability to strike second."8

Secretary of Defense Robert McNamara explained U.S. policy in 1968:

The cornerstone of our strategic policy continues to be to deter deliberate nuclear attack upon the United States or its allies. We do this by maintaining a highly reliable ability to inflict unacceptable damage upon any single aggressor or combination of aggressors at any time during the course of a strategic nuclear exchange, even after

absorbing a surprise first strike. This can be defined as our *assured-destruction capability*.
Assured destruction is the very essence of the whole deterrence concept. We must possess an actual assureddestruction capability, and that capability also must be credible. . . . If the United States is to deter a nuclear attack on itself or its allies, it must possess an actual and a credible assured-destruction capability.[9]

The key to such a capability was possession of secure retaliatory capabilities—that is, second-strike forces that could "ride out" the enemy's first strike and in turn inflict unacceptable damage on the enemy's homeland. Such capabilities would in essence make the enemy's first strike an act of national suicide. Continued McNamara:

When calculating the force required, we must be conservative in all our estimates of both a potential aggressor's capabilities and his intentions. Security depends on assuming a worst possible case, and having the ability to cope with it. In that eventuality we must be able to absorb the total weight of nuclear attack on our country—on our retaliatory forces, on our command and control apparatus, on our industrial capacity, on our cities, and on our population—and still be capable of damaging the aggressor to the point that his society would be simply no longer viable in twentieth-century terms. That is what deterrence of nuclear aggression means. It means the certainty of suicide to the aggressor, not merely to his military forces, but to his society as a whole.[10]

Chapter - 5

Peaceful use of nuclear energy

Nuclear technologies are used daily to find and protect sustainable sources of fresh water, produce

energy and food, while providing researchers the tools to study the ocean's past and predict its future. The IAEA helps its 154 member countries safely employ these technologies to ensure peace, health
and prosperity throughout the world.

" *Population growth, accelerating economic development, and changing lifestyles demand ever more resources.* Resource overuse has begun to compromise "natural services" such as biodiversity,
clean air, fresh water and arable land; a trend that threatens the sustainability of development. "Natural services" are inextricably interlinked. Decisions related to the management of a single resource impacts others.
Yet, today at the national level, future land, water and energy policies are usually planned by

separately operating institutions.

An integrated system is needed to bring decision-makers together to address the complex challenge of designing development policies for an uncertain future. Integrated solutions can resiliently adapt to a changing climate and the natural resource constraints that could exacerbate existing inequalities.

To help Member State governments achieve greater adaptability, the IAEA has developed a new methodology for modelling these complex interactions called CLEWS (Climate, Land-use, Energy and Water Strategies) that allows simultaneous and cohesive analysis of all these areas.

" *Increased access to sufficient, safe*

water is made possible through nuclear techniques that map ground water resources more affordably and more quickly than any other means, and thus improve water managers' ability to sustain this irreplaceable resource. Nuclear techniques enhance the efficiency of agricultural irrigation, which uses 70% of all freshwater resources.

" *Access to affordable energy* directly improves human welfare; current projections foresee electricity demand increasing by 60 to 100% between today and 2030. Low carbon sources of energy, such as nuclear energy, minimize the greenhouse gases emitted in energy generation and mitigate the negative impact of climatic disruption on development. The IAEA helps countries using or

introducing nuclear power to do
so safely, securely, economically
and sustainably. Its safety standards,
assistance and reviews
increase safety for the benefit of
human health and the environment.
The IAEA also verifies that
nuclear energy is only used for
peaceful purposes, directly contributing
to international
peace and security.

Young scientists come from IAEA Member States around the world to expand their knowledge through on-the-job training at MEL's advanced research facilities. Support for them is provided through IAEA Coordinated Research
Projects, Internships
and Technical Cooperation Fellowships.
Nineteen African countries are
now part of the IAEA´s
technical

cooperation project that aims to promote drip irrigation for high-value crops.

"*Access to sustainable sources of food* will remain a preeminent challenge in the decades to come. Based upon current practice and consumption, agricultural production will have to increase by about 70% by 2050 to meet demand. Nuclear techniques are used in developing countries to increase production sustainably by breeding improved crops, enhancing livestock reproduction and nutrition, as well as controlling animal and plant pests and diseases. Post-harvest losses can be reduced and safety increased with nuclear technology. Soil can be evaluated with nuclear techniques to conserve and improve soil productivity and water management.

" *To better understand and protect oceans,* nuclear techniques are used to monitor the ocean's shifting chemical balance caused by ocean acidification that can stunt and endanger coral and microorganisms' growth. This chemical shift can limit the habitats and disrupt the food chain for the species that supply up to a third of all protein consumed by humans. Nuclear techniques are also powerful tools used to acquire an accurate picture of the ocean's distant past. With an improved understanding of past climates, predictions about this enormous, life-sustaining realm's future will be more accurate.

" *Health for millions of patients relies upon the safe and effective diagnosis and treatment of disease.*

Nuclear techniques provide precise diagnostic information that is of vital importance in detecting and curing both infectious and non-communicable diseases such as cancer. Radiopharmaceuticals are used to treat disease and to enable diagnostic imaging.

Radiotherapy also employs focused radiation beams that are essential in curing diseases. In the developing world, infectious and non-communicable diseases, as well as malnutrition, create a socio-economic burden that threatens sustainability. The safe, well-coordinated use of nuclear techniques to detect, diagnose and treat disease and to combat malnutrition contributes to improved health and social stability throughout the world.

Nuclear Technology for a SUSTAINABLE FUTURE | 7

A SAFE OPERATING SPAC E FOR HUMANITY

Humans have become a major shaping force of the environment. This force that is fuelled by the growing demand for goods and services overexploits natural resources and ultimately leads to the degradation of natural ecosystems. Climate change amplifies the negative impact of our resource overuse. Measures, such as irrigation, desalination or the production of biofuels, that are designed to help mitigate and adapt to these climatic changes, are in themselves resource-intensive.

Current demand and resource use projections indicate that inclusive and sustainable development in the future is threatened.

The United Nations Sustainable Development Conference, Rio+20, may launch a process to better define a safe and more equitable operating space for humanity that defines how we can preserve the environmental services upon which future generations depend, as well as offering socio-economic opportunity for all.

Solutions for sustainability

The linkages among the agricultural,

water, energy and environmental sectors offer opportunities to apply nuclear technologies that provide solutions to these complex inter-related challenges. Crosssectoral planning increases the effectiveness with which resources are employed, providing an essential benefit that supports sustainability. For instance, appropriate planning, development and monitoring can ensure that crops are bred to deliver as much nutrition as possible while using as little water and land as possible. Or, careful analysis can identify linked constraints in food and bioenergy production as a result of water or land resource limitations.

A leading priority in low income countries' is to find the means to

enhance water, energy and food security, while contending with low resource productivity, in particular low agricultural yields, natural resource degradation, rapid population growth and weak institutional capacity. To help Member States develop integrated solutions for sustainable development challenges,
the IAEA has created a
tool that models these complex interactions called CLEWS (Climate, Land-use, Energy and Water Strategies).
CLEWS allows planners to conduct a simultaneous and cohesive analysis
of these systems.
Access to enough fresh, safe water is of paramount importance to ensure sustainable development. The IAEA helps Member States develop science-based information

and technical skills to improve their understanding and management of water resources.

By tracking the isotopes of water, scientists can quickly obtain valuable information that may otherwise require decades of hydrological data collection to gather. Working with partners in government and the United Nations system, the IAEA has been a pioneer in developing isotope hydrology as a powerful and effective scientific approach for managing water resources.

WATER

Today, one billion people have no access to safe drinking water, and only about 15% of the world's population enjoy relative abundance.

Unsafe water, carrying preventable, water-borne diseases, kills nearly five million people annually. Most victims of unsafe water are children. Rising populations, more irrigated agriculture and increasing industrial growth together deplete and degrade freshwater supplies faster than these can be replenished. In addition, river flows have become more variable and vulnerable in a warmer climate (due to increased glacial melt and changes in precipitation patterns). These concurrent trends are driving the need to optimize water use and management practices.

Water's fingerprints

Through its technical cooperation projects, the IAEA works with Member States to tackle water pollution and scarcity issues. For instance, to be able to depend upon fresh water supplies in the future, Member States must be able to accurately measure the available water resources. Water contains varying concentrations of naturallyoccurring isotopes that can be measured with nuclear techniques. The measurements identify a specific water sample's origin precisely, quickly, easily and costeffectively. The isotopic composition of water serves as a 'fingerprint' that allows researchers to track where water travels from its origin, what happens to water along its course and how quickly it is being replenished. Isotope tracking also helps researchers detect sources of pollution and salt water intrusion, and identify the effects of climate change.

IAEA water resource projects are in operation in Africa, Asia, Europe and Latin America, addressing a variety of groundwater and surface water resource challenges. For example, a study conducted by the

IAEA in Bangladesh — where naturally-occurring arsenic poisoning created a major public health crisis — uncovered the source of contamination and provided information about where to find safe drinking water.

Reliance on aquifers

More than half the world's population relies on water pumped from aquifers, many of which traverse national boundaries. Nuclear methods rapidly and reliably map transboundary aquifers, producing the data needed to plan how to share the water sustainably, rationally and equitably. The IAEA is studying several major underground aquifers, such as the Nubian Sandstone Aquifer System in Africa and the Guarani aquifer in South America. These projects support better

groundwater resource management, which is the basis for sustainable socio-economic development, as well as the preservation of biodiversity
and land resources.

How much water is available?

The IAEA's Water Availability Enhancement Project (IWAVE) strengthens Member States' national capacity to conduct water resource assessments by identifying gaps in hydrological data and formulating strategies to close them.

These comprehensive assessments include evaluations of water quality, water quantity, and water use, as well as resource vulnerability and sustainability. This information will complement other international, regional, and national initiatives to provide decision makers reliable tools to better manage national water resources. IWAVE pilot studies are under way in Costa Rica, Oman and the Philippines.

Cooperation is the key to sustainable water supplies

Developing countries receive training and technical analytical support in nuclear technology through the IAEA hydrology projects, as well as expert services and equipment. The IAEA Isotope Hydrology Laboratory offers analytical support and services to ensure high-quality isotope measurements worldwide, and helps Member States establish their own laboratories. The IAEA's newsletters, atlases, on-line applications, training programmes, e-learning, and isotope information help water resource managers make effective decisions. To strengthen the impact and broaden the reach of its programmes, the IAEA works together with other organizations, such as the World Bank, United Nations Environment Programme, Organization of American States and United States Geological Survey to facilitate programmes and transfer knowledge.

The IAEA is also a member of UN Water, an inter-agency group that brings together 30 United Nations organizations collaborating on effective fresh water management.

ENERGY

Development that relieves poverty relies upon access to energy. *Sustainable* development relies upon access to clean, sufficient and affordable energy. Globally, about 1.3 billion people, have no access to electricity, and are deprived of the opportunities that energy enables in education, agriculture, business,

industry, and healthcare. Half of the world's population has no access to clean cooking fuels, relying instead on biomass such as wood, dung and agricultural residue, as well as coal, to fuel cook stoves and to heat their homes. The WHO estimates that diseases caused by the resulting
indoor air pollution kill
two million people annually.

Energy choices

Expanding energy access requires systematic planning to find the optimal combination of sources that deliver energy that is affordable, while conserving resources and protecting the environment. For the rural poor, off-grid renewable energy may offer the greatest promise. For the urban poor and growing mega-cities, the energy mix must include large, centralized electricity generation facilities to meet large-scale, centralized electricity demand.

The IAEA is the sole UN agency involved in overall capacity building in energy system analysis. It offers a comprehensive menu of support to assist developing countries plan for their future energy needs. Under the IAEA energy planning approach, all energy options are treated equally. Together with national planners, the IAEA develops and transfers tailored planning models and data that consider all of the economic, environmental, and social aspects of sustainable development. The IAEA trains local experts and establishes local capacity to chart national energy paths for sustainable development.

The IAEA is a founding member of UN-Energy, a network that promotes coherence within the United Nations family of organizations in the energy field and develops engagement between the United Nations and other key external stakeholders

Using nuclear power safely

To be a viable contributor to sustainable development, nuclear power must be safe: accidents must be prevented and avoided; the emergency response must ensure that any radioactive release is minimized and swiftly stopped to prevent public exposure. The IAEA's safety standards, safety training, direct assistance and safety peer reviews help ensure that the highest safety levels are in place.

After the Fukushima-Daiichi nuclear power plant accident the IAEA's Member States approved an Action Plan on Nuclear Safety. The Action Plan focuses a global effort to strengthen nuclear safety worldwide. Under the Action Plan, all countries with nuclear power programs agreed to promptly undertake nuclear power plant 'stress tests'. The IAEA's peer reviews are being strengthened by incorporating lessons learned from the accident and by ensuring that these reviews appropriately address regulatory effectiveness, operational safety, design safety, and emergency preparedness and response.

Essential to all human activities, energy fuels social and economic development.
Energy is the engine for the production of goods and services across all economic
sectors: agriculture, industry, transportation, commerce, public administration,
among many others. Lack of energy is a contributing factor in individual, community, national and regional poverty. In contrast, access to energy opens many new opportunities;
and meeting the United Nations Millennium Development Goals cannot be accomplished without access to affordable energy services.

Using nuclear power economically and sustainably

Nuclear power is not a panacea. It is a good investment if the benefits exceed the risks, costs less than available alternatives, pays for itself, and results in profitable operation. Ensuring profitability requires good planning, infrastructure and operation.

For countries that choose to introduce nuclear power, the IAEA provides guidance and assistance in developing the necessary legislative and regulatory framework, human resources, nuclear safety, stakeholder involvement, emergency planning, environmental protection, non-proliferation safeguards and nuclear waste management.

When a nation includes nuclear power in its energy mix, it reduces harmful air pollution and greenhouse gas emissions, expands electricity supplies, increases the national stock of technological and human capital and broadens the resource base by putting uranium to productive use.

Due to its environmental risk, radioactive
waste requires special attention. The IAEA, as the only UN organization involved in radioactive

waste management, establishes safety standards and provides technical and related guidance for the implementation of waste management in accordance with those safety standards.

Using nuclear power securely

As with safety, nuclear power must be secured against malicious acts such as sabotage, theft or attacks to be a viable contributor to sustainable development. The IAEA develops security guidelines and provides training, direct assistance and peer reviews to ensure that security is maintained at the highest possible levels.

Using nuclear power peacefully

Sustainable development depends upon international peace and security, which the IAEA helps to maintain by verifying that nuclear power is used for peaceful purposes only. This is essential because, unlike other energy forms, nuclear energy can be misused to pursue military purposes and develop nuclear weapons.

Over the past five decades, the international community has put in place a number of international legal mechanisms to help stem the spread of nuclear weapons. These include the Treaty on the Non-Proliferation of Nuclear Weapons and the IAEA safeguards system. The IAEA applies safeguards, a set of technical measures through which it independently verifies that nuclear material is not diverted from peaceful uses. The IAEA plays an important verification role, demonstrating
to States that
nuclear non-proliferation

commitments are being respected.

Nuclear Technology for a SUSTAINABLE FUTURE | 11

FOOD SECURITY AND SUSTAINABLE AGRICULTURE

As the effects of a changing climate become more evident, many countries are burdened by longer drought periods, flood-triggered soil erosion, encroaching saline water, and the devastation wrought by extreme weather. All of these factors can severely constrain food production and sustainable development. Nuclear techniques are used to increase crop and soil productivity, efficiently manage water resources,

improve livestock health and productivity
and reduce the use of fertilizers.

Healthier livestock

Healthy and productive livestock help ensure food security. Nuclear techniques are used to improve livestock growth, reproductive efficiency and disease resistance. For instance, radioimmunoassay methods help diagnose diseases and monitor the effectiveness of disease control and eradication programmes. This methodology is essential in stopping the spread of trans-boundary animal diseases, such as rinderpest, which was recently completely eradicated worldwide.

Defence against insect pests

Nuclear techniques can be used as part of an integrated approach to control insect pests that destroy crops and spread disease. Diseases and pests destroy more than a third of crops before and after harvesting. Insect pests can be controlled using the sterile insect technique (SIT). In SIT, an environmentally friendly alternative to insecticides, male, laboratory-raised insects, are sterilized with gamma radiation. When they are released into the wild and mate, no offspring are produced. Over time, insect populations shrink and are eventually fully suppressed, reducing the need for pesticides. SIT has been used to eradicate the medfly, a threat to some 250 species of fruit and vegetables,
from Chile and Mexico, as well as from parts of Guatemala and the United States.

Reducing pollutants

By suppressing insect pest populations with SIT, pesticide use worldwide had been reduced by 600 000 litres annually. At the same time, the technique has improved incomes for 18 000 producers, since these pesticide-free products, grown in developing countries, satisfy international food safety requirements, thereby increasing the access of rural agricultural communities to valuable export markets. For example, the use of SIT in Guatemala reduced the fruit fly population, which helped double earnings from the agricultural export of tomatoes, bell peppers and papaya, while providing badly needed new jobs. Since 2006, the insect pest control programme has generated benefits to farmers of more than $100 million and created thousands of rural jobs.

Plant breeding

For instance, when seeds are briefly

exposed to radiation, subtle genetic changes in plants occur, speeding up a natural process that would otherwise take many years. The IAEA utilizes this technique to help Member States swiftly develop commercial crops that are more resistant to disease or drought. A wide range of improved crop varieties, such as rice, wheat, banana, potato, yam and soya bean, have been developed. These varieties are now planted for instance on 15% of Vietnam's rice production area, where they have been adopted as part of a national programme to "eradicate hunger and alleviate poverty", focussing on the central highland region, an economically
poor area where agricultural production is low. These techniques expand the range of productive
land and increase the

global food supply.

Services to ensure food security

Through a joint programme, the Food and Agriculture Organization and the IAEA collaborate to support global food security and contribute to combatting poverty. IAEA services increase Member States' capacity to adapt to climate change by offering needs assessments, technical advice, training, coordinated research projects, equipment, networking, technical publications and public information.

PROTECTING THE OCEANS

The IAEA's Environment Laboratories in Monaco help Member States apply nuclear techniques
to detect pollutants in coastal zones and the deep ocean,

analyse their impacts on marine organisms and human health, and better understand key marine heat and carbon cycling processes.

Ocean acidification

The oceans absorb 2 billion tonnes of carbon dioxide every year, and act as a powerful buffer that mitigates the effects of global warming. The IAEA Environmental Laboratories study ocean acidification and climate
change's other effects on oceans and marine ecosystems. Ocean acidification occurs as oceans absorb the rising quantities of carbon
dioxide in the atmosphere. When dissolved, the carbon dioxide forms carbonic acid, creating a more acidic environment, which can threaten marine ecosystems. Corals and other marine organisms, particularly

those with shells, are at particular risk. The IAEA is using radiotracers to track the effects of this acidification on ocean chemistry and marine life. This knowledge is needed to be able to act effectively to protect the oceans that are the primary source of food for more than 3.5 billion people.

To support international efforts to mitigate ocean acidification, the IAEA, together with UNESCO and 155 scientists, drafted and signed the 2009 Monaco Declaration, which calls for substantial reductions in CO_2 emissions to avoid widespread damage to marine ecosystems caused by ocean acidification. The IAEA is an active member of UN Oceans, which is an effective, interagency coordination mechanism on ocean and coastal issues within the United Nations.

Understanding climate change

The IAEA contributes to basic climate science by using nuclear techniques to learn more about past climates. The isotopic "natural archives" preserved in marine sediments, ice cores, corals and polar ice offer a wealth of information. The isotope record provides precise data about the environmental conditions on Earth over the past millennia. Information about the ocean's temperature, salinity, acidity, humidity, biodiversity, and circulation in the ancient past helps scientists verify the accuracy of current ocean and climate models and helps orient future model development. These models are needed to predict the ocean's "health" and the weather in future.

Preventing marine pollution

The IAEA has worked with several regional organizations to improve their capacity to use nuclear techniques to monitor and assess marine pollutants, like heavy metals and pesticides. Projects to enhance the capability of Black Sea and Caribbean countries to assess and monitor coastal pollution problems have been successfully completed. In the Caribbean and the Philippines, nuclear techniques have been validated as reliable, swift, cost-effective tools that detect toxins produced by harmful algal blooms in marine foods.

Measuring marine radioactive pollution

The IAEA's Environment Laboratories have provided essential scientific and analytical support for a landmark study of radioactive and non-radioactive pollutant levels in all principal seas. They have undertaken worldwide radioactivity baseline studies of the Antarctic, Arctic, Atlantic, Indian, North and South Pacific Oceans, and the Far Eastern, Mediterranean, and Black Seas. Regional studies have been conducted in the Gulf, as well as the Caspian, Irish, and Kara Seas, in addition to the New Caledonia, Mururoa and Fangataufa Atolls. The baselines levels are essential for identifying changes to the radioactivity levels in the marine environment.

Following the Fukushima Daiichi nuclear accident, radioactively contaminated cooling water was discharged into the sea, raising concern about the radioactivity's harmful effects on marine life and on seafood destined for human and animal consumption. Japan initiated

an intense programme to
monitor both coastal and off-shore
levels of seawater contamination at
the discharge area, as well as at distances
10 and 30 kilometers from
the reactors. The IAEA is now undertaking
a long-term marine study of
the Pacific through an IAEA regional
cooperation project.

HUMAN HEALTH

In developing countries, malnutrition,
communicable and non-communicable
diseases, particularly
cancer, threaten health and cut
short productive lives. Health
problems
and diseases

can be detected and treated using nuclear techniques.

Fighting non-communicable diseases

Non-communicable diseases, such as cardiovascular diseases, cancer, diabetes and chronic lung disease, are a significant barrier to sustainable development. The WHO estimates that the costly, long term health-care needed to treat these diseases consumes family savings in low and middle-income countries and drives about 100 million people into poverty every year. More than 36 million people are killed each year by these diseases, and nearly 80% of these deaths occur in lowand middle-income countries. A quarter of the victims die early, before their sixtieth birthday, often robbing families of a breadwinner.

For over 40 years, the IAEA has helped its Member States to build sustainable capacity in the use of radiation medicine and has assisted more than 110 low and middleincome countries to manage cancer and non-communicable diseases. For instance, with the assistance of the IAEA, Mauritania's first radiotherapy centre was inaugurated in 2010, and, cancer patients are receiving treatment in their home country. Another IAEA project in Yemen has helped to establish the necessary infrastructure for the country's first nuclear medicine centre,
by building the necessary human capacity, training staff and providing essential equipment, such as a double-head gamma camera. The Nuclear Medicine Centre at Al-Thawra Hospital was opened in early 2008 and can provide services

to many of the 23 000 patients per year requiring cancer, renal and cardiology diagnosis, and serves as a national training centre in Yemen.

Fighting cancer in the developing world

Today, most new cancer cases are diagnosed in the developing world where access to cancer diagnosis and treatment is very limited. According to the WHO, more than two-thirds of new cases and cancer deaths — almost eight million people worldwide per year — occur in low and middle income countries. Cancer is spreading in these countries at an epidemic rate. Cancer, which often affects the most productive working-age members of society, could become a major impediment to socio-economic development in low and middle income countries.

Radiotherapy: a cancer-fighter's essential tool

The WHO considers radiation therapy to be "fundamental to the optimum management of cancer patients", which alone, or in combination with surgery or chemotherapy, is recommended for more than half of cancer patients. Radiotherapy is attractive for developing countries, because it is a highly cost-effective option for cancer treatment.

In 2004, the IAEA established the Programme of Action for Cancer Therapy (PACT) to help fight cancer in its developing Member States comprehensively and effectively, through partnerships and resource mobilization. PACT builds upon the IAEA's expertise in radiation medicine technology to enable low and middle income countries to introduce, expand and improve their cancer care services and workforce. PACT also conducts missions to evaluate Member States' readiness to implement cancer control programmes and offer recommendations on developing cancer control capacity.

Global alliance

The WHO/IAEA Joint Programme on Cancer Control is a global alliance of NGOs, foundations, public and multilateral organisations and private industry that works to increase awareness, build technical and public policy capacity and develop alternative fundraising mechanisms to help establish much needed national cancer control programmes in developing countries. With the support of the WHO/IAEA Joint Programme, countries such as Ghana now have established a national cancer control plan, and are implementing infrastructure improvements and developing the needed workforce, which all are helping to improve the health of the population in the country.

Improving nutrition

Malnutrition has devastating humanitarian and economic consequences, contributing to developmental problems and weakened immune systems, and to subsequent long term impacts on the economy. One out of every ten children born in developing countries will die before their fifth birthday as a result of malnutrition. According to the World Bank, investing in infant and young child nutrition can save one million lives each year, and can help 260 million more children and their mothers have a healthier future. Given its comparatively low cost, investing in children's improved nutrition is one of the most effective interventions to advance sustainability. The IAEA's nutrition programme, in cooperation with WHO and UNICEF, uses nuclear techniques to monitor a wide variety of nutritional problems. To improve breastfeeding practices, manage healthy growth and address micro-nutrient deficiencies, the IAEA helps Member States develop effective, evidencebased interventions to combat malnutrition using stable isotope and other nuclear techniques. These methods are non-radioactive and non-invasive procedures. For the first time, this method is being used in fifteen African countries to collect a large data set on human milk intake and the prevalence of exclusive breastfeeding. Nuclear techniques are also used for neonatal screening for sickle cell disease, hypothyroidism and cystic fibrosis, as well as childhood cancers.

GHANA — Cassava variety 'Tek Bankye', with improved cooking quality, released to wide acclaim. Trials underway to produce higher-yielding, disease resistant cassava, with improved starch content.

CANADA — The Linola mutant series of linseed is similar to traditional sunflower oil and therefore suitable for human consumption. Linola accounts for about 10% of all flax/linseed grown in Canada, a major flax producer.

CAPACITY BUILDING

At the heart of the IAEA's activities is building local capacity
through technology transfer. Working with its Member
States, the IAEA's role is to make sure that this technology is
used safely and effectively, and can also be locally sustained.
This means providing training to develop local expertise and
ensuring that any needed infrastructure is in place before
technology is transferred.

The IAEA helps Member States develop scientific and technical
capacities in water management, soil management,
agriculture,
energy planning, nuclear engineering, and environmental
and climate research to enhance sustainability

nationally and regionally. As a result, many developing countries
are using state-of-the-art nuclear science and technology
to solve chronic developmental challenges, such as
ensuring public health, providing sufficient energy, food and
fresh water, as well as preserving a safe environment. The
IAEA's services include expert needs assessments, technical
advice, training, equipment procurement, networking, technical
publications and public information, which are delivered
through coordinated research projects and the technical cooperation programme.
The IAEA helps countries that choose to introduce nuclear
power to make the necessary long-term plans, to develop
the necessary infrastructure and to continuously improve

safety and efficiency, and provides guidance on each of the milestones that a country must meet when preparing for nuclear power. These milestones distil lessons from past experience, helping countries that choose to introduce nuclear power today to do so safely, securely and sustainably.

The IAEA helps countries to assess their progress against the milestones and provides training and assistance to strengthen their programmes and speed their progress.

Over the past five decades, the IAEA and its Member States have built a sound foundation of institutions and personnel in many developing countries that now provide an important regional resource — in terms of capabilities and expertise.

Today, developing countries are better positioned to use
nuclear science and technology to improve public health,
provide sufficient food, energy and water; and sustain a safe
environment.
By advancing the peaceful uses of nuclear technologies, the
IAEA helps its Member States address basic human development
needs, while building the future we want.

VIETNAM — Since the mid-1990s eight mutant rice varieties were
released, with high quality, increased yield and tolerance to soil
salinity. Since 2000, the area cultivated with mutant rice varieties
reached 2.5 million hectares in southern Vietnam.

SUDAN — Banana variety 'Albeely' producing up to 100% higher
yields and improved quality.

www.iaea.org

Chapter - 6

CTBT

COMPREHENSIVE NUCLEAR-TEST-BAN TREATY

PREAMBLE

The States Parties to this Treaty (hereinafter referred
to as "the States Parties"),

Welcoming the international agreements and other
positive measures of recent years in the field of nuclear
disarmament, including reductions in arsenals of nuclear
weapons, as well as in the field of the prevention of nuclear
proliferation in all its aspects,

Underlining the importance of the full and prompt

implementation of such agreements and measures,

Convinced that the present international situation provides an opportunity to take further effective measures towards nuclear disarmament and against the proliferation of nuclear weapons in all its aspects, and declaring their intention to take such measures,

Stressing therefore the need for continued systematic and progressive efforts to reduce nuclear weapons globally, with the ultimate goal of eliminating those weapons, and of

general and complete disarmament under strict and effective international control,

Recognizing that the cessation of all nuclear weapon

test explosions and all other nuclear explosions, by
constraining the development and qualitative improvement
of nuclear weapons and ending the development of
advanced new types of nuclear weapons, constitutes an
effective measure of nuclear disarmament and nonproliferation
in all its aspects,
Further recognizing that an end to all such nuclear
explosions will thus constitute a meaningful step in the
realization of a systematic process to achieve nuclear
disarmament,
Convinced that the most effective way to achieve an
end to nuclear testing is through the conclusion of a
universal and internationally and effectively verifiable

comprehensive nuclear test-ban treaty, which has long
been one of the highest priority objectives of the
international community in the field of disarmament and
non-proliferation,

Noting the aspirations expressed by the Parties to the
1963 Treaty Banning Nuclear Weapon Tests in the

Atmosphere, in Outer Space and Under Water to seek to
achieve the discontinuance of all test explosions of nuclear
weapons for all time,

Noting also the views expressed that this Treaty could contribute to the protection of the environment,

Affirming the purpose of attracting the adherence of
all States to this Treaty and its objective to contribute

effectively to the prevention of the proliferation of nuclear weapons in all its aspects, to the process of nuclear disarmament and therefore to the enhancement of international peace and security,

Have agreed as follows:

ARTICLE I
BASIC OBLIGATIONS

1. Each State Party undertakes not to carry out any nuclear weapon test explosion or any other nuclear explosion, and to prohibit and prevent any such nuclear explosion at any place under its jurisdiction or control.

2. Each State Party undertakes, furthermore, to refrain from causing, encouraging, or in any way participating in the

carrying out of any nuclear weapon test explosion or any
other nuclear explosion.

ARTICLE II

THE ORGANIZATION

A. GENERAL PROVISIONS

1. The States Parties hereby establish the Comprehensive Nuclear Test-Ban Treaty Organization (hereinafter referred to as "the Organization") to achieve the object and purpose of this Treaty, to ensure the implementation of its provisions, including those for international verification of compliance with it, and to provide a forum for consultation and cooperation among States Parties.

2. All States Parties shall be members of the Organization. A State Party shall not be deprived of its membership in the Organization.

3. The seat of the Organization shall be Vienna, Republic of Austria.

4. There are hereby established as organs of the Organization: the Conference of the States Parties, the Executive Council and the Technical Secretariat, which shall include the International Data Centre.

5. Each State Party shall cooperate with the Organization in the exercise of its functions in accordance with this Treaty. States Parties shall consult, directly among themselves, or through the Organization or other appropriate international procedures, including procedures within the framework of the United Nations and in accordance with its Charter, on any matter which may be raised relating to the object and purpose, or the

implementation of the provisions, of this Treaty.

6. The Organization shall conduct its verification activities provided for under this Treaty in the least intrusive manner possible consistent with the timely and efficient accomplishment of their objectives. It shall request only the information and data necessary to fulfil its responsibilities under this Treaty. It shall take every precaution to protect the confidentiality of information on civil and military activities and facilities coming to its knowledge in the implementation of this Treaty and, in particular, shall abide by the confidentiality provisions set forth in this Treaty.

7. Each State Party shall treat as confidential and afford

special handling to information and data that it receives in confidence from the Organization in connection with the implementation of this Treaty. It shall treat such information and data exclusively in connection with its rights and obligations under this Treaty.

8. The Organization, as an independent body, shall seek to utilize existing expertise and facilities, as appropriate, and to maximize cost efficiencies, through cooperative arrangements with other international organizations such as the International Atomic Energy Agency. Such arrangements, excluding those of a minor and normal commercial and contractual nature, shall be set

out in agreements to be submitted to the Conference of the States Parties for approval.

9. The costs of the activities of the Organization shall be met annually by the States Parties in accordance with the United Nations scale of assessments adjusted to take into account differences in membership between the United Nations and the Organization.

10. Financial contributions of States Parties to the Preparatory Commission shall be deducted in an appropriate way from their contributions to the regular budget.

11. A member of the Organization which is in arrears in the payment of its assessed contribution to the Organization

shall have no vote in the Organization if the amount of its arrears equals or exceeds the amount of the contribution due from it for the preceding two full years. The Conference of the States Parties may, nevertheless, permit such a member to vote if it is satisfied that the failure to pay is due to conditions beyond the control of the member.

B. THE CONFERENCE OF THE STATES PARTIES

Composition, Procedures and Decision-making

12. The Conference of the States Parties (hereinafter referred to as "the Conference") shall be composed of all States Parties. Each State Party shall have one representative in the Conference, who may be accompanied by alternates and advisers.

13. The initial session of the Conference shall be

convened by the Depositary no later than 30 days after the entry into force of this Treaty.

14. The Conference shall meet in regular sessions, which shall be held annually, unless it decides otherwise.

15. A special session of the Conference shall be convened:

(a) When decided by the Conference;
(b) When requested by the Executive Council; or
(c) When requested by any State Party and supported by a majority of the States Parties. The special session shall be convened no later than 30 days after the decision of the Conference, the request of the Executive Council, or the attainment of the necessary support, unless specified otherwise in the decision or request.

16. The Conference may also be convened in the form of an Amendment Conference, in accordance with Article VII.

17. The Conference may also be convened in the form of a Review Conference, in accordance with Article VIII.

18. Sessions shall take place at the seat of the Organization unless the Conference decides otherwise.

19. The Conference shall adopt its rules of procedure. At the beginning of each session, it shall elect its President and such other officers as may be required. They shall hold office until a new President and other officers are elected at the next session.

20. A majority of the States Parties shall constitute a quorum.

21. Each State Party shall have one vote.
22. The Conference shall take decisions on matters of procedure by a majority of members present and voting. Decisions on matters of substance shall be taken as far as possible by consensus. If consensus is not attainable when an issue comes up for decision, the President of the Conference shall defer any vote for 24 hours and during this period of deferment shall make every effort to facilitate achievement of consensus, and shall report to the Conference before the end of this period. If consensus is not possible at the end of 24 hours, the Conference shall take a decision by a two-thirds majority of members present

and voting unless specified otherwise in this Treaty. When
the issue arises as to whether the question is one of
substance or not, that question shall be treated as a matter
of substance unless otherwise decided by the majority
required for decisions on matters of substance.

23. When exercising its function under paragraph 26 (k),
the Conference shall take a decision to add any State to the
list of States contained in Annex 1 to this Treaty in
accordance with the procedure for decisions on matters of
substance set out in paragraph 22. Notwithstanding
paragraph 22, the Conference shall take decisions on any
other change to Annex 1 to this Treaty by consensus.

Powers and Functions

24. The Conference shall be the principal organ of the Organization. It shall consider any questions, matters or issues within the scope of this Treaty, including those relating to the powers and functions of the Executive Council and the Technical Secretariat, in accordance with this Treaty. It may make recommendations and take decisions on any questions, matters or issues within the scope of this Treaty raised by a State Party or brought to its attention by the Executive Council.

25. The Conference shall oversee the implementation of, and review compliance with, this Treaty and act in order to

promote its object and purpose. It shall also oversee the activities of the Executive Council and the Technical Secretariat and may issue guidelines to either of them for the exercise of their functions.

26. The Conference shall:

(a) Consider and adopt the report of the Organization on the implementation of this Treaty and the annual programme and budget of the Organization, submitted by the Executive Council, as well as consider other reports;

(b) Decide on the scale of financial contributions to be paid by States Parties in accordance with paragraph 9;

(c) Elect the members of the Executive Council;

(d) Appoint the Director-General of the Technical

Secretariat (hereinafter referred to as "the Director-
General");

(e) Consider and approve the rules of procedure of
the Executive Council submitted by the latter;

(f) Consider and review scientific and technological
developments that could affect the operation of this Treaty.
In this context, the Conference may direct the
Director-General to establish a Scientific Advisory Board to
enable him or her, in the performance of his or her
functions, to render specialized advice in areas of science
and technology relevant to this Treaty to the Conference, to
the Executive Council, or to States Parties. In that case, the
Scientific Advisory Board shall be composed of independent

experts serving in their individual capacity and appointed, in accordance with terms of reference adopted by the Conference, on the basis of their expertise and experience in the particular scientific fields relevant to the implementation of this Treaty;

(g) Take the necessary measures to ensure compliance with this Treaty and to redress and remedy any situation that contravenes the provisions of this Treaty, in accordance with Article V;

(h) Consider and approve at its initial session any draft agreements, arrangements, provisions, procedures, operational manuals, guidelines and any other documents developed and recommended by the Preparatory Commission;

(i) Consider and approve agreements or arrangements negotiated by the Technical Secretariat with
States Parties, other States and international organizations
to be concluded by the Executive Council on behalf of the
Organization in accordance with paragraph 38 (h);
(j) Establish such subsidiary organs as it finds necessary for the exercise of its functions in accordance
with this Treaty; and
(k) Update Annex 1 to this Treaty, as appropriate,
in accordance with paragraph 23.

C. THE EXECUTIVE COUNCIL

Composition, Procedures and Decision-making

27. The Executive Council shall consist of 51 members.
Each State Party shall have the right, in accordance with
the provisions of this Article, to serve on the Executive

Council.

28. Taking into account the need for equitable geographical distribution, the Executive Council shall
comprise:

(a) Ten States Parties from Africa;
(b) Seven States Parties from Eastern Europe;
(c) Nine States Parties from Latin America and the
Caribbean;
(d) Seven States Parties from the Middle East and
South Asia;
(e) Ten States Parties from North America and Western Europe; and
(f) Eight States Parties from South-East Asia, the Pacific and the Far East.

All States in each of the above geographical regions are
listed in Annex 1 to this Treaty. Annex 1 to this Treaty shall
be updated, as appropriate, by the Conference in

accordance with paragraphs 23 and 26 (k). It shall not be subject to amendments or changes under the procedures contained in Article VII.

29. The members of the Executive Council shall be elected by the Conference. In this connection, each geographical region shall designate States Parties from that region for election as members of the Executive Council as follows:

(a) At least one-third of the seats allocated to each geographical region shall be filled, taking into account political and security interests, by States Parties in that region designated on the basis of the nuclear capabilities relevant to the Treaty as determined by international data as well as all or any of the following indicative criteria in the order of priority determined by each region:

(i) Number of monitoring facilities of the International Monitoring System;

(ii) Expertise and experience in monitoring technology; and

(iii) Contribution to the annual budget of the Organization;

(b) One of the seats allocated to each geographical region shall be filled on a rotational basis by the State Party that is first in the English alphabetical order among the States Parties in that region that have not served as members of the Executive Council for the longest period of time since becoming States Parties or since their last term, whichever is shorter. A State Party designated on this basis may decide to forgo its seat. In that case, such a State Party shall submit a letter of renunciation to the Director-General, and the seat shall be filled by the State Party following next-in-order according to this sub-paragraph; and

(c) The remaining seats allocated to each geographical region shall be filled by States Parties designated from among all the States Parties in that region by rotation or elections.

30. Each member of the Executive Council shall have one representative on the Executive Council, who may be accompanied by alternates and advisers.

31. Each member of the Executive Council shall hold

office from the end of the session of the Conference at which that member is elected until the end of the second regular annual session of the Conference thereafter, except that for the first election of the Executive Council, 26 members shall be elected to hold office until the end of the third regular annual session of the Conference, due regard being paid to the established numerical proportions as described in paragraph 28.

32. The Executive Council shall elaborate its rules of procedure and submit them to the Conference for approval.

33. The Executive Council shall elect its Chairman from among its members.

34. The Executive Council shall meet for regular

sessions. Between regular sessions it shall meet as may be required for the fulfilment of its powers and functions.

35. Each member of the Executive Council shall have one vote.

36. The Executive Council shall take decisions on matters of procedure by a majority of all its members. The Executive Council shall take decisions on matters of substance by a two-thirds majority of all its members unless specified otherwise in this Treaty. When the issue arises as to whether the question is one of substance or not, that question shall be treated as a matter of substance unless otherwise decided by the majority required for decisions on matters of substance.

Powers and Functions

37. The Executive Council shall be the executive organ of the Organization. It shall be responsible to the Conference.

It shall carry out the powers and functions entrusted to it in accordance with this Treaty. In so doing, it shall act in conformity with the recommendations, decisions and guidelines of the Conference and ensure their continuous and proper implementation.

38. The Executive Council shall:

(a) Promote effective implementation of, and compliance with, this Treaty;

(b) Supervise the activities of the Technical Secretariat;

(c) Make recommendations as necessary to the Conference for consideration of further proposals for promoting the object and purpose of this Treaty;

(d) Cooperate with the National Authority of each State Party;

(e) Consider and submit to the Conference the draft annual programme and budget of the Organization, the draft report of the Organization on the implementation of this Treaty, the report on the performance of its own activities and such other reports as it deems necessary or that the Conference may request;

(f) Make arrangements for the sessions of the Conference, including the preparation of the draft agenda;

(g) Examine proposals for changes, on matters of an administrative or technical nature, to the Protocol or the

Annexes thereto, pursuant to Article VII, and make recommendations to the States Parties regarding their adoption;

(h) Conclude, subject to prior approval of the Conference, agreements or arrangements with States Parties, other States and international organizations on behalf of the Organization and supervise their implementation, with the exception of agreements or arrangements referred to in sub-paragraph (i);

(i) Approve and supervise the operation of agreements or arrangements relating to the implementation

of verification activities with States Parties and other States; and

(j) Approve any new operational manuals and any

changes to the existing operational manuals that may be proposed by the Technical Secretariat.

39. The Executive Council may request a special session of the Conference.

40. The Executive Council shall:

(a) Facilitate cooperation among States Parties, and between States Parties and the Technical Secretariat, relating to the implementation of this Treaty through information exchanges;

(b) Facilitate consultation and clarification among States Parties in accordance with Article IV; and

(c) Receive, consider and take action on requests for, and reports on, on-site inspections in accordance with Article IV.

41. The Executive Council shall consider any concern

raised by a State Party about possible non-compliance with
this Treaty and abuse of the rights established by this
Treaty. In so doing, the Executive Council shall consult with
the States Parties involved and, as appropriate, request a
State Party to take measures to redress the situation within
a specified time. To the extent that the Executive Council
considers further action to be necessary, it shall take, inter
alia, one or more of the following measures:
(a) Notify all States Parties of the issue or matter;
(b) Bring the issue or matter to the attention of the
Conference;
(c) Make recommendations to the Conference or

take action, as appropriate, regarding measures to redress the situation and to ensure compliance in accordance with Article V.

D. THE TECHNICAL SECRETARIAT

42. The Technical Secretariat shall assist States Parties in the implementation of this Treaty. The Technical Secretariat shall assist the Conference and the Executive Council in the performance of their functions. The Technical Secretariat shall carry out the verification and other functions entrusted to it by this Treaty, as well as those functions delegated to it by the Conference or the Executive Council in accordance with this Treaty. The Technical Secretariat shall include, as an integral part, the

International Data Centre.

43. The functions of the Technical Secretariat with regard to verification of compliance with this Treaty shall, in accordance with Article IV and the Protocol, include inter alia:

(a) Being responsible for supervising and coordinating the operation of the International Monitoring System;

(b) Operating the International Data Centre;

(c) Routinely receiving, processing, analysing and reporting on International Monitoring System data;

(d) Providing technical assistance in, and support for, the installation and operation of monitoring stations;

(e) Assisting the Executive Council in facilitating

consultation and clarification among States Parties;

(f) Receiving requests for on-site inspections and processing them, facilitating Executive Council consideration of such requests, carrying out the preparations for, and providing technical support during, the conduct of on-site inspections, and reporting to the Executive Council;

(g) Negotiating agreements or arrangements with States Parties, other States and international organizations and concluding, subject to prior approval by the Executive Council, any such agreements or arrangements relating to verification activities with States Parties or other States; and

(h) Assisting the States Parties through their National Authorities on other issues of verification under this

Treaty.

44. The Technical Secretariat shall develop and maintain, subject to approval by the Executive Council, operational manuals to guide the operation of the various components of the verification regime, in accordance with Article IV and the Protocol. These manuals shall not constitute integral parts of this Treaty or the Protocol and may be changed by the Technical Secretariat subject to approval by the Executive Council. The Technical Secretariat shall promptly inform the States Parties of any changes in the operational manuals.

45. The functions of the Technical Secretariat with respect to administrative matters shall include:

(a) Preparing and submitting to the Executive Council the draft programme and budget of the Organization;
(b) Preparing and submitting to the Executive Council the draft report of the Organization on the implementation of this Treaty and such other reports as the Conference or the Executive Council may request;
(c) Providing administrative and technical support to the Conference, the Executive Council and other subsidiary organs;
(d) Addressing and receiving communications on behalf of the Organization relating to the implementation of this Treaty; and
(e) Carrying out the administrative responsibilities

related to any agreements between the Organization and
other international organizations.

46. All requests and notifications by States Parties to the
Organization shall be transmitted through their National
Authorities to the Director-General. Requests and
notifications shall be in one of the official languages of this
Treaty. In response the Director-General shall use the
language of the transmitted request or notification.

47. With respect to the responsibilities of the Technical
Secretariat for preparing and submitting to the Executive
Council the draft programme and budget of the
Organization, the Technical Secretariat shall determine and
maintain a clear accounting of all costs for each facility

established as part of the International Monitoring System.

Similar treatment in the draft programme and budget shall be accorded to all other activities of the Organization.

48. The Technical Secretariat shall promptly inform the Executive Council of any problems that have arisen with regard to the discharge of its functions that have come to its notice in the performance of its activities and that it has been unable to resolve through consultations with the State Party concerned.

49. The Technical Secretariat shall comprise a Director-General, who shall be its head and chief administrative officer, and such scientific, technical and

other personnel as may be required. The Director-General
shall be appointed by the Conference upon the recommendation of the Executive Council for a term of four
years, renewable for one further term, but not thereafter.
The first Director-General shall be appointed by the
Conference at its initial session upon the recommendation
of the Preparatory Commission.

50. The Director-General shall be responsible to the
Conference and the Executive Council for the appointment
of the staff and for the organization and functioning of the
Technical Secretariat. The paramount consideration in the
employment of the staff and in the determination of the
conditions of service shall be the necessity of securing the

highest standards of professional expertise, experience, efficiency, competence and integrity. Only citizens of States Parties shall serve as the Director-General, as inspectors or as members of the professional and clerical staff. Due regard shall be paid to the importance of recruiting the staff on as wide a geographical basis as possible. Recruitment shall be guided by the principle that the staff shall be kept to the minimum necessary for the proper discharge of the responsibilities of the Technical Secretariat.

51. The Director-General may, as appropriate, after consultation with the Executive Council, establish temporary working groups of scientific experts to provide recommendations on specific issues.

52. In the performance of their duties, the Director-General, the inspectors, the inspection assistants and the members of the staff shall not seek or receive instructions from any Government or from any other source external to the Organization. They shall refrain from any action that might reflect adversely on their positions as international officers responsible only to the Organization. The Director-General shall assume responsibility for the activities of an inspection team.

53. Each State Party shall respect the exclusively international character of the responsibilities of the Director-General, the inspectors, the inspection assistants and the members of the staff and shall not seek to influence them in the discharge of their responsibilities.

E. PRIVILEGES AND IMMUNITIES

54. The Organization shall enjoy on the territory and in any other place under the jurisdiction or control of a State Party such legal capacity and such privileges and immunities as are necessary for the exercise of its functions.

55. Delegates of States Parties, together with their alternates and advisers, representatives of members elected to the Executive Council, together with their alternates and advisers, the Director-General, the inspectors, the inspection assistants and the members of the staff of the Organization shall enjoy such privileges and immunities as are necessary in the independent exercise of

their functions in connection with the Organization.

56. The legal capacity, privileges and immunities referred to in this Article shall be defined in agreements between the Organization and the States Parties as well as in an agreement between the Organization and the State in which the Organization is seated. Such agreements shall be considered and approved in accordance with paragraph 26 (h) and (i).

-30-

57. Notwithstanding paragraphs 54 and 55, the privileges and immunities enjoyed by the Director-General, the inspectors, the inspection assistants and the members of the staff of the Technical Secretariat during the conduct of

verification activities shall be those set forth in the Protocol.

ARTICLE III
NATIONAL IMPLEMENTATION MEASURES

1. Each State Party shall, in accordance with its constitutional processes, take any necessary measures to implement its obligations under this Treaty. In particular, it shall take any necessary measures:

(a) To prohibit natural and legal persons anywhere on its territory or in any other place under its jurisdiction as recognized by international law from undertaking any activity prohibited to a State Party under this Treaty;

(b) To prohibit natural and legal persons from undertaking any such activity anywhere under its control; and

(c) To prohibit, in conformity with international law,
natural persons possessing its nationality from undertaking
any such activity anywhere.
2. Each State Party shall cooperate with other States
Parties and afford the appropriate form of legal assistance
to facilitate the implementation of the obligations under
paragraph 1.
3. Each State Party shall inform the Organization of the
measures taken pursuant to this Article.
4. In order to fulfil its obligations under the Treaty, each
State Party shall designate or set up a National Authority
and shall so inform the Organization upon entry into force of
the Treaty for it. The National Authority shall serve as the

national focal point for liaison with the Organization and with other States Parties.

ARTICLE IV
VERIFICATION

A. GENERAL PROVISIONS

1. In order to verify compliance with this Treaty, a verification regime shall be established consisting of the following elements:

(a) An International Monitoring System;
(b) Consultation and clarification;
(c) On-site inspections; and
(d) Confidence-building measures.

At entry into force of this Treaty, the verification regime shall be capable of meeting the verification requirements of this Treaty.

2. Verification activities shall be based on objective

information, shall be limited to the subject matter of this Treaty, and shall be carried out on the basis of full respect

for the sovereignty of States Parties and in the least intrusive manner possible consistent with the effective and timely accomplishment of their objectives. Each State Party shall refrain from any abuse of the right of verification.

3. Each State Party undertakes in accordance with this Treaty to cooperate, through its National Authority established pursuant to Article III, paragraph 4, with the Organization and with other States Parties to facilitate the verification of compliance with this Treaty by, inter alia:

(a) Establishing the necessary facilities to

participate in these verification measures and establishing
the necessary communication;
(b) Providing data obtained from national stations
that are part of the International Monitoring System;
(c) Participating, as appropriate, in a consultation
and clarification process;
(d) Permitting the conduct of on-site inspections;
and
(e) Participating, as appropriate, in confidence-
-35-
building measures.
4. All States Parties, irrespective of their technical and
financial capabilities, shall enjoy the equal right of
verification and assume the equal obligation to accept
verification.

5. For the purposes of this Treaty, no State Party shall
be precluded from using information obtained by national
technical means of verification in a manner consistent with
generally recognized principles of international law,
including that of respect for the sovereignty of States.

6. Without prejudice to the right of States Parties to
protect sensitive installations, activities or locations not
related to this Treaty, States Parties shall not interfere with
elements of the verification regime of this Treaty or with
national technical means of verification operating in
accordance with paragraph 5.

7. Each State Party shall have the right to take measures to protect sensitive installations and to prevent

disclosure of confidential information and data not related to this Treaty.

8. Moreover, all necessary measures shall be taken to protect the confidentiality of any information related to civil and military activities and facilities obtained during verification activities.

9. Subject to paragraph 8, information obtained by the Organization through the verification regime established by this Treaty shall be made available to all States Parties in accordance with the relevant provisions of this Treaty and the Protocol.

10. The provisions of this Treaty shall not be interpreted as restricting the international exchange of data for scientific

purposes.

11. Each State Party undertakes to cooperate with the Organization and with other States Parties in the improvement of the verification regime, and in the examination of the verification potential of additional monitoring technologies such as electromagnetic pulse monitoring or satellite monitoring, with a view to developing, when appropriate, specific measures to enhance the efficient and cost-effective verification of this Treaty. Such measures shall, when agreed, be incorporated in existing provisions in this Treaty, the Protocol or as additional sections of the Protocol, in accordance with Article VII, or, if

appropriate, be reflected in the operational manuals in accordance with Article II, paragraph 44.

12. The States Parties undertake to promote cooperation among themselves to facilitate and participate in the fullest possible exchange relating to technologies used in the verification of this Treaty in order to enable all States Parties to strengthen their national implementation of verification measures and to benefit from the application of such technologies for peaceful purposes.

13. The provisions of this Treaty shall be implemented in a manner which avoids hampering the economic and technological development of the States Parties for further development of the application of atomic energy for peaceful

purposes.

Verification Responsibilities of the Technical Secretariat

14. In discharging its responsibilities in the area of verification specified in this Treaty and the Protocol, in cooperation with the States Parties the Technical Secretariat shall, for the purpose of this Treaty:

(a) Make arrangements to receive and distribute data and reporting products relevant to the verification of this Treaty in accordance with its provisions, and to maintain a global communications infrastructure appropriate to this task;

(b) Routinely through its International Data Centre, which shall in principle be the focal point within the

Technical Secretariat for data storage and data processing:

(i) Receive and initiate requests for data from the International Monitoring System;

(ii) Receive data, as appropriate, resulting from the process of consultation and clarification, from on-site inspections, and from confidence-building measures; and

(iii) Receive other relevant data from States Parties and international organizations in accordance with this Treaty and the Protocol;

(c) Supervise, coordinate and ensure the operation of the International Monitoring System and its component elements, and of the International Data Centre, in accordance with the relevant operational manuals;

(d) Routinely process, analyse and report on International Monitoring System data according to agreed

procedures so as to permit the effective international
verification of this Treaty and to contribute to the early
resolution of compliance concerns;

(e) Make available all data, both raw and processed, and any reporting products, to all States Parties, each State Party taking responsibility for the use of International Monitoring System data in accordance with Article II, paragraph 7, and with paragraphs 8 and 13 of this Article;

(f) Provide to all States Parties equal, open, convenient and timely access to all stored data;

(g) Store all data, both raw and processed, and reporting products;

(h) Coordinate and facilitate requests for additional data from the International Monitoring System;

(i) Coordinate requests for additional data from one
State Party to another State Party;

(j) Provide technical assistance in, and support for,
the installation and operation of monitoring facilities and
respective communication means, where such assistance
and support are required by the State concerned;

(k) Make available to any State Party, upon its request, techniques utilized by the Technical Secretariat
and its International Data Centre in compiling, storing,
processing, analysing and reporting on data from the
verification regime; and

(l) Monitor, assess and report on the overall performance of the International Monitoring System and of
the International Data Centre.

15. The agreed procedures to be used by the Technical Secretariat in discharging the verification responsibilities referred to in paragraph 14 and detailed in the Protocol shall be elaborated in the relevant operational manuals.

B. THE INTERNATIONAL MONITORING SYSTEM

16. The International Monitoring System shall comprise facilities for seismological monitoring, radionuclide monitoring including certified laboratories, hydroacoustic monitoring, infrasound monitoring, and respective means of communication, and shall be supported by the International Data Centre of the Technical Secretariat.

17. The International Monitoring System shall be placed

under the authority of the Technical Secretariat. All monitoring facilities of the International Monitoring System shall be owned and operated by the States hosting or otherwise taking responsibility for them in accordance with the Protocol.

18. Each State Party shall have the right to participate in the international exchange of data and to have access to all data made available to the International Data Centre. Each State Party shall cooperate with the International Data Centre through its National Authority.

Funding the International Monitoring System

19. For facilities incorporated into the International Monitoring System and specified in Tables 1-A, 2-A, 3 and 4

of Annex 1 to the Protocol, and for their functioning, to the extent that such facilities are agreed by the relevant State
and the Organization to provide data to the International
Data Centre in accordance with the technical requirements
of the Protocol and relevant operational manuals, the
Organization, as specified in agreements or arrangements
pursuant to Part I, paragraph 4 of the Protocol, shall meet
the costs of:
(a) Establishing any new facilities and upgrading existing facilities, unless the State responsible for such
facilities meets these costs itself;
(b) Operating and maintaining International Monitoring System facilities, including facility physical

security if appropriate, and application of agreed data
authentication procedures;

(c) Transmitting International Monitoring System
data (raw or processed) to the International Data Centre by
the most direct and cost-effective means available,
including, if necessary, via appropriate communications
nodes, from monitoring stations, laboratories, analytical
facilities or from national data centres; or such data
(including samples where appropriate) to laboratory and
analytical facilities from monitoring stations; and

(d) Analysing samples on behalf of the Organization.

20. For auxiliary network seismic stations specified in

Table 1-B of Annex 1 to the Protocol the Organization, as
specified in agreements or arrangements pursuant to Part I,
paragraph 4 of the Protocol, shall meet the costs only of:
(a) Transmitting data to the International Data Centre;
(b) Authenticating data from such stations;
(c) Upgrading stations to the required technical standard, unless the State responsible for such facilities
meets these costs itself;
(d) If necessary, establishing new stations for the
purposes of this Treaty where no appropriate facilities
currently exist, unless the State responsible for such
facilities meets these costs itself; and
(e) Any other costs related to the provision of data
required by the Organization as specified in the relevant

operational manuals.

21. The Organization shall also meet the cost of provision to each State Party of its requested selection from the standard range of International Data Centre reporting products and services, as specified in Part I, Section F of the Protocol. The cost of preparation and transmission of any additional data or products shall be met by the requesting State Party.

22. The agreements or, if appropriate, arrangements concluded with States Parties or States hosting or otherwise taking responsibility for facilities of the International Monitoring System shall contain provisions for meeting

these costs. Such provisions may include modalities
whereby a State Party meets any of the costs referred to in
paragraphs 19 (a) and 20 (c) and (d) for facilities which it
hosts or for which it is responsible, and is compensated by
an appropriate reduction in its assessed financial
contribution to the Organization. Such a reduction shall not
exceed 50 per cent of the annual assessed financial
contribution of a State Party, but may be spread over
successive years. A State Party may share such a reduction with another State Party by agreement or
arrangement between themselves and with the concurrence
of the Executive Council. The agreements or arrangements

referred to in this paragraph shall be approved in accordance with Article II, paragraphs 26 (h) and 38 (i).

Changes to the International Monitoring System

23. Any measures referred to in paragraph 11 affecting the International Monitoring System by means of addition or deletion of a monitoring technology shall, when agreed, be incorporated into this Treaty and the Protocol pursuant to Article VII, paragraphs 1 to 6.

24. The following changes to the International Monitoring System, subject to the agreement of those States directly affected, shall be regarded as matters of an administrative or technical nature pursuant to Article VII, paragraphs 7 and 8:

(a) Changes to the number of facilities specified in
the Protocol for a given monitoring technology; and
(b) Changes to other details for particular facilities
as reflected in the Tables of Annex 1 to the Protocol
(including, inter alia, State responsible for the facility;
location; name of facility; type of facility; and attribution of a
facility between the primary and auxiliary seismic networks).

If the Executive Council recommends, pursuant to Article
VII, paragraph 8 (d), that such changes be adopted, it shall
as a rule also recommend pursuant to Article VII, paragraph
8 (g), that such changes enter into force upon notification by
the Director-General of their approval.

25. The Director-General, in submitting to the Executive Council and States Parties information and evaluation in accordance with Article VII, paragraph 8 (b), shall include in the case of any proposal made pursuant to paragraph 24:

(a) A technical evaluation of the proposal;

(b) A statement on the administrative and financial impact of the proposal; and

(c) A report on consultations with States directly affected by the proposal, including indication of their agreement.

Temporary Arrangements

26. In cases of significant or irretrievable breakdown of a monitoring facility specified in the Tables of Annex 1 to the Protocol, or in order to cover other temporary reductions of

monitoring coverage, the Director-General shall, in consultation and agreement with those States directly affected, and with the approval of the Executive Council, initiate temporary arrangements of no more than one year's duration, renewable if necessary by agreement of the Executive Council and of the States directly affected for another year. Such arrangements shall not cause the number of operational facilities of the International Monitoring System to exceed the number specified for the relevant network; shall meet as far as possible the technical and operational requirements specified in the operational manual for the relevant network; and shall be conducted within the budget of the Organization. The Director-General shall furthermore take steps to rectify the situation and make proposals for its permanent resolution. The Director-General shall notify all States Parties of any decision taken pursuant to this paragraph.

Cooperating National Facilities

27. States Parties may also separately establish cooperative arrangements with the Organization, in order to make available to the International Data Centre supplementary data from national monitoring stations that are not formally part of the International Monitoring System.

28. Such cooperative arrangements may be established as follows:

(a) Upon request by a State Party, and at the

expense of that State, the Technical Secretariat shall take
the steps required to certify that a given monitoring facility
meets the technical and operational requirements specified
in the relevant operational manuals for an International
Monitoring System facility, and make arrangements for the
authentication of its data. Subject to the agreement of the
Executive Council, the Technical Secretariat shall then
formally designate such a facility as a cooperating national
facility. The Technical Secretariat shall take the steps
required to revalidate its certification as appropriate;

(b) The Technical Secretariat shall maintain a current list of cooperating national facilities and shall distribute it to all States Parties; and

(c) The International Data Centre shall call upon data from cooperating national facilities, if so requested by a State Party, for the purposes of facilitating consultation and clarification and the consideration of on-site inspection requests, data transmission costs being borne by that State Party.

-49-

The conditions under which supplementary data from such facilities are made available, and under which the International Data Centre may request further or expedited reporting, or clarifications, shall be elaborated in the operational manual for the respective monitoring network.

C. CONSULTATION AND CLARIFICATION

29. Without prejudice to the right of any State Party to

request an on-site inspection, States Parties should, whenever possible, first make every effort to clarify and resolve, among themselves or with or through the Organization, any matter which may cause concern about possible non-compliance with the basic obligations of this Treaty.

30. A State Party that receives a request pursuant to paragraph 29 directly from another State Party shall provide the clarification to the requesting State Party as soon as possible, but in any case no later than 48 hours after the request. The requesting and requested States Parties may keep the Executive Council and the Director-General informed of the request and the response.

31. A State Party shall have the right to request the Director-General to assist in clarifying any matter which may cause concern about possible non-compliance with the basic obligations of this Treaty. The Director-General shall provide appropriate information in the possession of the Technical Secretariat relevant to such a concern. The Director-General shall inform the Executive Council of the request and of the information provided in response, if so requested by the requesting State Party.

32. A State Party shall have the right to request the Executive Council to obtain clarification from another State Party on any matter which may cause concern about

possible non-compliance with the basic obligations of this
Treaty. In such a case, the following shall apply:
(a) The Executive Council shall forward the request
for clarification to the requested State Party through the
Director-General no later than 24 hours after its receipt;
(b) The requested State Party shall provide the clarification to the Executive Council as soon as possible,
but in any case no later than 48 hours after receipt of the
request;
(c) The Executive Council shall take note of the
clarification and forward it to the requesting State Party no
later than 24 hours after its receipt;
(d) If the requesting State Party deems the clarification to be inadequate, it shall have the right to

request the Executive Council to obtain further clarification
from the requested State Party. The Executive Council shall inform without delay all other
States Parties about any request for clarification pursuant to
this paragraph as well as any response provided by the
requested State Party.

33. If the requesting State Party considers the clarification obtained under paragraph 32 (d) to be
unsatisfactory, it shall have the right to request a meeting of
the Executive Council in which States Parties involved that
are not members of the Executive Council shall be entitled
to take part. At such a meeting, the Executive Council shall
consider the matter and may recommend any measure in
accordance with Article V.

D. ON-SITE INSPECTIONS

Request for an On-Site Inspection

34. Each State Party has the right to request an on-site inspection in accordance with the provisions of this Article and Part II of the Protocol in the territory or in any other place under the jurisdiction or control of any State Party, or in any area beyond the jurisdiction or control of any State.

35. The sole purpose of an on-site inspection shall be to clarify whether a nuclear weapon test explosion or any other nuclear explosion has been carried out in violation of Article I and, to the extent possible, to gather any facts which might assist in identifying any possible violator.

36. The requesting State Party shall be under the

obligation to keep the on-site inspection request within the scope of this Treaty and to provide in the request information in accordance with paragraph 37. The requesting State Party shall refrain from unfounded or abusive inspection requests.

37. The on-site inspection request shall be based on information collected by the International Monitoring System, on any relevant technical information obtained by national technical means of verification in a manner consistent with generally recognized principles of international law, or on a combination thereof. The request shall contain information pursuant to Part II, paragraph 41 of

the Protocol.

38. The requesting State Party shall present the on-site inspection request to the Executive Council and at the same time to the Director-General for the latter to begin immediate processing.

Follow-up After Submission of an On-Site Inspection Request

39. The Executive Council shall begin its consideration immediately upon receipt of the on-site inspection request.

40. The Director-General, after receiving the on-site inspection request, shall acknowledge receipt of the request to the requesting State Party within two hours and communicate the request to the State Party sought to be

inspected within six hours. The Director-General shall
ascertain that the request meets the requirements specified
in Part II, paragraph 41 of the Protocol, and, if necessary,

-54-

shall assist the requesting State Party in filing the request
accordingly, and shall communicate the request to the
Executive Council and to all other States Parties within 24
hours.

41. When the on-site inspection request fulfils the
requirements, the Technical Secretariat shall begin
preparations for the on-site inspection without delay.

42. The Director-General, upon receipt of an on-site
inspection request referring to an

42. The Director-General, upon receipt of an on-site inspection request referring to an inspection area under the jurisdiction or control of a State Party, shall immediately seek clarification from the State Party sought to be inspected in order to clarify and resolve the concern raised in the request.

43. A State Party that receives a request for clarification pursuant to paragraph 42 shall provide the Director-General with explanations and with other relevant information available as soon as possible, but no later than 72 hours after receipt of the request for clarification.

44. The Director-General, before the Executive Council takes a decision on the on-site inspection request, shall transmit immediately to the Executive Council any additional information available from the International Monitoring System or provided by any State Party on the event specified in the request, including any clarification provided pursuant to paragraphs 42 and 43, as well as any other

information from within the Technical Secretariat that the Director-General deems relevant or that is requested by the Executive Council.

45. Unless the requesting State Party considers the concern raised in the on-site inspection request to be resolved and withdraws the request, the Executive Council shall take a decision on the request in accordance with paragraph 46.

Executive Council Decisions

46. The Executive Council shall take a decision on the on-site inspection request no later than 96 hours after receipt of the request from the requesting State Party. The decision to approve the on-site inspection shall be made by

at least 30 affirmative votes of members of the Executive Council. If the Executive Council does not approve the inspection, preparations shall be stopped and no further action on the request shall be taken.

47. No later than 25 days after the approval of the on-site inspection in accordance with paragraph 46, the inspection team shall transmit to the Executive Council, through the Director-General, a progress inspection report. The continuation of the inspection shall be considered approved unless the Executive Council, no later than 72 hours after receipt of the progress inspection report, decides by a majority of all its members not to continue the inspection. If

the Executive Council decides not to continue the inspection, the inspection shall be terminated, and the inspection team shall leave the inspection area and the territory of the inspected State Party as soon as possible in accordance with Part II, paragraphs 109 and 110 of the Protocol.

48. In the course of the on-site inspection, the inspection team may submit to the Executive Council, through the Director-General, a proposal to conduct drilling. The Executive Council shall take a decision on such a proposal no later than 72 hours after receipt of the proposal. The decision to approve drilling shall be made by a majority of all members of the Executive Council.

49. The inspection team may request the Executive Council, through the Director-General, to extend the inspection duration by a maximum of 70 days beyond the 60-day time-frame specified in Part II, paragraph 4 of the Protocol, if the inspection team considers such an extension essential to enable it to fulfil its mandate. The inspection team shall indicate in its request which of the activities and techniques listed in Part II, paragraph 69 of the Protocol it intends to carry out during the extension period. The Executive Council shall take a decision on the extension request no later than 72 hours after receipt of the request.

The decision to approve an extension of the inspection duration shall be made by a majority of all members of the Executive Council.

50. Any time following the approval of the continuation of the on-site inspection in accordance with paragraph 47, the inspection team may submit to the Executive Council, through the Director-General, a recommendation to terminate the inspection. Such a recommendation shall be considered approved unless the Executive Council, no later than 72 hours after receipt of the recommendation, decides by a two-thirds majority of all its members not to approve the termination of the inspection. In case of termination of

the inspection, the inspection team shall leave the
inspection area and the territory of the inspected State Party
as soon as possible in accordance with Part II,
paragraphs 109 and 110 of the Protocol.

51. The requesting State Party and the State Party
sought to be inspected may participate in the deliberations
of the Executive Council on the on-site inspection request
without voting. The requesting State Party and the
inspected State Party may also participate without voting in
any subsequent deliberations of the Executive Council
related to the inspection.

52. The Director-General shall notify all States Parties
within 24 hours about any decision by and reports,

proposals, requests and recommendations to the Executive
Council pursuant to paragraphs 46 to 50.

Follow-up After Executive Council Approval of an On-Site Inspection

53. An on-site inspection approved by the Executive
Council shall be conducted without delay by an inspection
team designated by the Director-General and in accordance
with the provisions of this Treaty and the Protocol. The
inspection team shall arrive at the point of entry no later
than six days following the receipt by the Executive Council
of the on-site inspection request from the requesting State
Party.

54. The Director-General shall issue an inspection

mandate for the conduct of the on-site inspection. The inspection mandate shall contain the information specified in Part II, paragraph 42 of the Protocol.

55. The Director-General shall notify the inspected State Party of the inspection no less than 24 hours before the planned arrival of the inspection team at the point of entry, in accordance with Part II, paragraph 43 of the Protocol.

The Conduct of an On-Site Inspection

56. Each State Party shall permit the Organization to conduct an on-site inspection on its territory or at places under its jurisdiction or control in accordance with the provisions of this Treaty and the Protocol. However, no State Party shall have to accept simultaneous on-site

inspections on its territory or at places under its jurisdiction
or control.

57. In accordance with the provisions of this Treaty and
the Protocol, the inspected State Party shall have:

(a) The right and the obligation to make every reasonable effort to demonstrate its compliance with this
Treaty and, to this end, to enable the inspection team to fulfil
its mandate;

(b) The right to take measures it deems necessary
to protect national security interests and to prevent
disclosure of confidential information not related to the
purpose of the inspection;

(c) The obligation to provide access within the inspection area for the sole purpose of determining facts relevant to the purpose of the inspection, taking into account sub-paragraph (b) and any constitutional obligations it may have with regard to proprietary rights or searches and seizures;

(d) The obligation not to invoke this paragraph or Part II, paragraph 88 of the Protocol to conceal any violation of its obligations under Article I; and

(e) The obligation not to impede the ability of the inspection team to move within the inspection area and to carry out inspection activities in accordance with this Treaty and the Protocol.

Access, in the context of an on-site inspection, means both the physical access of the inspection team and the

inspection equipment to, and the conduct of inspection
activities within, the inspection area.

58. The on-site inspection shall be conducted in the least
intrusive manner possible, consistent with the efficient and
timely accomplishment of the inspection mandate, and in
accordance with the procedures set forth in the Protocol.
Wherever possible, the inspection team shall begin with the
least intrusive procedures and then proceed to more
intrusive procedures only as it deems necessary to collect
sufficient information to clarify the concern about possible
non-compliance with this Treaty. The inspectors shall seek
only the information and data necessary for the purpose of

the inspection and shall seek to minimize interference with normal operations of the inspected State Party.

59. The inspected State Party shall assist the inspection team throughout the on-site inspection and facilitate its task.

60. If the inspected State Party, acting in accordance with Part II, paragraphs 86 to 96 of the Protocol, restricts access within the inspection area, it shall make every reasonable effort in consultations with the inspection team to demonstrate through alternative means its compliance with this Treaty.

Observer

61. With regard to an observer, the following shall apply:

(a) The requesting State Party, subject to the

agreement of the inspected State Party, may send a representative, who shall be a national either of the requesting State Party or of a third State Party, to observe the conduct of the on-site inspection;

(b) The inspected State Party shall notify its acceptance or non-acceptance of the proposed observer to the Director-General within 12 hours after approval of the on-site inspection by the Executive Council;

(c) In case of acceptance, the inspected State Party shall grant access to the observer in accordance with the Protocol;

(d) The inspected State Party shall, as a rule, accept the proposed observer, but if the inspected State Party exercises a refusal, that fact shall be recorded in the inspection report.

There shall be no more than three observers from an aggregate of requesting States Parties.

Reports of an On-Site Inspection

62. Inspection reports shall contain:

(a) A description of the activities conducted by the inspection team;

(b) The factual findings of the inspection team relevant to the purpose of the inspection;

(c) An account of the cooperation granted during the on-site inspection;

(d) A factual description of the extent of the access granted, including the alternative means provided to the team, during the on-site inspection; and

(e) Any other details relevant to the purpose of the inspection.

Differing observations made by inspectors may be attached

to the report.

63. The Director-General shall make draft inspection reports available to the inspected State Party. The inspected State Party shall have the right to provide the Director-General within 48 hours with its comments and explanations, and to identify any information and data which, in its view, are not related to the purpose of the inspection and should not be circulated outside the Technical Secretariat. The Director-General shall consider the proposals for changes to the draft inspection report made by the inspected State Party and shall wherever possible incorporate them. The Director-General shall also

annex the comments and explanations provided by the inspected State Party to the inspection report.

64. The Director-General shall promptly transmit the inspection report to the requesting State Party, the inspected State Party, the Executive Council and to all other States Parties. The Director-General shall further transmit promptly to the Executive Council and to all other States Parties any results of sample analysis in designated laboratories in accordance with Part II, paragraph 104 of the Protocol, relevant data from the International Monitoring System, the assessments of the requesting and inspected States Parties, as well as any other information that the

Director-General deems relevant. In the case of the
progress inspection report referred to in paragraph 47, the
Director-General shall transmit the report to the Executive
Council within the time-frame specified in that paragraph.

65. The Executive Council, in accordance with its powers
and functions, shall review the inspection report and any
material provided pursuant to paragraph 64, and shall
address any concerns as to:

(a) Whether any non-compliance with this Treaty
has occurred; and

(b) Whether the right to request an on-site inspection has been abused.

66. If the Executive Council reaches the conclusion, in

keeping with its powers and functions, that further action may be necessary with regard to paragraph 65, it shall take the appropriate measures in accordance with Article V.

Frivolous or Abusive On-Site Inspection Requests

67. If the Executive Council does not approve the on-site inspection on the basis that the on-site inspection request is frivolous or abusive, or if the inspection is terminated for the same reasons, the Executive Council shall consider and

decide on whether to implement appropriate measures to redress the situation, including the following:

(a) Requiring the requesting State Party to pay for the cost of any preparations made by the Technical

Secretariat;
(b) Suspending the right of the requesting State Party to request an on-site inspection for a period of time,
as determined by the Executive Council; and
(c) Suspending the right of the requesting State Party to serve on the Executive Council for a period of time.

E. CONFIDENCE-BUILDING MEASURES

68. In order to:
(a) Contribute to the timely resolution of any compliance concerns arising from possible misinterpretation
of verification data relating to chemical explosions; and
(b) Assist in the calibration of the stations that are
part of the component networks of the International
Monitoring System,

each State Party undertakes to cooperate with the

Organization and with other States Parties in implementing relevant measures as set out in Part III of the Protocol.

ARTICLE V

MEASURES TO REDRESS A SITUATION AND TO ENSURE COMPLIANCE, INCLUDING SANCTIONS

1. The Conference, taking into account, inter alia, the recommendations of the Executive Council, shall take the necessary measures, as set forth in paragraphs 2 and 3, to ensure compliance with this Treaty and to redress and remedy any situation which contravenes the provisions of this Treaty.

2. In cases where a State Party has been requested by the Conference or the Executive Council to redress a

situation raising problems with regard to its compliance and
fails to fulfil the request within the specified time, the
Conference may, inter alia, decide to restrict or suspend the
State Party from the exercise of its rights and privileges
under this Treaty until the Conference decides otherwise.

3. In cases where damage to the object and purpose of
this Treaty may result from non-compliance with the basic
obligations of this Treaty, the Conference may recommend
to States Parties collective measures which are in
conformity with international law.

4. The Conference, or alternatively, if the case is urgent,
the Executive Council, may bring the issue, including

relevant information and conclusions, to the attention of the
United Nations.

ARTICLE VI
SETTLEMENT OF DISPUTES

1. Disputes that may arise concerning the application or the interpretation of this Treaty shall be settled in accordance with the relevant provisions of this Treaty and in conformity with the provisions of the Charter of the United Nations.

2. When a dispute arises between two or more States Parties, or between one or more States Parties and the Organization, relating to the application or interpretation of this Treaty, the parties concerned shall consult together with

a view to the expeditious settlement of the dispute by negotiation or by other peaceful means of the parties' choice, including recourse to appropriate organs of this Treaty and, by mutual consent, referral to the International Court of Justice in conformity with the Statute of the Court. The parties involved shall keep the Executive Council informed of actions being taken.

3. The Executive Council may contribute to the settlement of a dispute that may arise concerning the application or interpretation of this Treaty by whatever means it deems appropriate, including offering its good offices, calling upon the States Parties to a dispute to seek

a settlement through a process of their own choice, bringing
the matter to the attention of the Conference and
recommending a time-limit for any agreed procedure.

4. The Conference shall consider questions related to
disputes raised by States Parties or brought to its attention
by the Executive Council. The Conference shall, as it finds
necessary, establish or entrust organs with tasks related to
the settlement of these disputes in conformity with Article II,
paragraph 26 (j).

5. The Conference and the Executive Council are
separately empowered, subject to authorization from the
General Assembly of the United Nations, to request the
International Court of Justice to give an advisory opinion on

any legal question arising within the scope of the activities
of the Organization. An agreement between the Organization and the United Nations shall be concluded for
this purpose in accordance with Article II, paragraph 38 (h).

6. This Article is without prejudice to Articles IV and V.

ARTICLE VII
AMENDMENTS

1. At any time after the entry into force of this Treaty,
any State Party may propose amendments to this Treaty,
the Protocol, or the Annexes to the Protocol. Any State
Party may also propose changes, in accordance with
paragraph 7, to the Protocol or the Annexes thereto.
Proposals for amendments shall be subject to the

procedures in paragraphs 2 to 6. Proposals for changes, in
accordance with paragraph 7, shall be subject to the
procedures in paragraph 8.

2. The proposed amendment shall be considered and
adopted only by an Amendment Conference.

3. Any proposal for an amendment shall be communicated to the Director-General, who shall circulate it
to all States Parties and the Depositary and seek the views
of the States Parties on whether an Amendment
Conference should be convened to consider the proposal.
If a majority of the States Parties notify the Director-General
no later than 30 days after its circulation that they support
further consideration of the proposal, the Director-General

shall convene an Amendment Conference to which all
States Parties shall be invited.

4. The Amendment Conference shall be held immediately following a regular session of the Conference unless all States Parties that support the convening of an Amendment Conference request that it be held earlier. In no case shall an Amendment Conference be held less than 60 days after the circulation of the proposed amendment.

5. Amendments shall be adopted by the Amendment Conference by a positive vote of a majority of the States Parties with no State Party casting a negative vote.

6. Amendments shall enter into force for all States Parties 30 days after deposit of the instruments of

ratification or acceptance by all those States Parties casting
a positive vote at the Amendment Conference.
7. In order to ensure the viability and effectiveness of
this Treaty, Parts I and III of the Protocol and Annexes 1
and 2 to the Protocol shall be subject to changes in
accordance with paragraph 8, if the proposed changes are
related only to matters of an administrative or technical
nature. All other provisions of the Protocol and the Annexes
thereto shall not be subject to changes in accordance with
paragraph 8.
8. Proposed changes referred to in paragraph 7 shall be
made in accordance with the following procedures:
(a) The text of the proposed changes shall be

transmitted together with the necessary information to the Director-General. Additional information for the evaluation of the proposal may be provided by any State Party and the Director-General. The Director-General shall promptly communicate any such proposals and information to all States Parties, the Executive Council and the Depositary;

(b) No later than 60 days after its receipt, the Director-General shall evaluate the proposal to determine all its possible consequences for the provisions of this Treaty and its implementation and shall communicate any such information to all States Parties and the Executive Council;

(c) The Executive Council shall examine the proposal in the light of all information available to it, including whether the proposal fulfils the requirements of paragraph 7. No later than 90 days after its receipt, the Executive Council shall notify its recommendation, with appropriate explanations, to all States Parties for consideration. States Parties shall acknowledge receipt within 10 days;

(d) If the Executive Council recommends to all States Parties that the proposal be adopted, it shall be considered approved if no State Party objects to it within 90 days after receipt of the recommendation. If the Executive Council recommends that the proposal be rejected, it shall be considered rejected if no State Party objects to the rejection within 90 days after receipt of the recommendation;

(e) If a recommendation of the Executive Council
does not meet with the acceptance required under subparagraph
(d), a decision on the proposal, including whether
it fulfils the requirements of paragraph 7, shall be taken as a
matter of substance by the Conference at its next session;

(f) The Director-General shall notify all States Parties and the Depositary of any decision under this paragraph;

(g) Changes approved under this procedure shall
enter into force for all States Parties 180 days after the date
of notification by the Director-General of their approval
unless another time period is recommended by the

Executive Council or decided by the Conference.

ARTICLE VIII
REVIEW OF THE TREATY

1. Unless otherwise decided by a majority of the States Parties, ten years after the entry into force of this Treaty a Conference of the States Parties shall be held to review the operation and effectiveness of this Treaty, with a view to assuring itself that the objectives and purposes in the Preamble and the provisions of the Treaty are being realized. Such review shall take into account any new scientific and technological developments relevant to this Treaty. On the basis of a request by any State Party, the Review Conference shall consider the possibility of

permitting the conduct of underground nuclear explosions
for peaceful purposes. If the Review Conference decides
by consensus that such nuclear explosions may be
permitted, it shall commence work without delay, with a view
to recommending to States Parties an appropriate
amendment to this Treaty that shall preclude any military
benefits of such nuclear explosions. Any such proposed
amendment shall be communicated to the Director-General
by any State Party and shall be dealt with in accordance
with the provisions of Article VII.

2. At intervals of ten years thereafter, further Review
Conferences may be convened with the same objective, if

the Conference so decides as a matter of procedure in the
preceding year. Such Conferences may be convened after
an interval of less than ten years if so decided by the
Conference as a matter of substance.

3. Normally, any Review Conference shall be held
immediately following the regular annual session of the
Conference provided for in Article II.

ARTICLE IX
DURATION AND WITHDRAWAL

1. This Treaty shall be of unlimited duration.
2. Each State Party shall, in exercising its national
sovereignty, have the right to withdraw from this Treaty if it
decides that extraordinary events related to the subject
matter of this Treaty have jeopardized its supreme interests.

3. Withdrawal shall be effected by giving notice six months in advance to all other States Parties, the Executive Council, the Depositary and the United Nations Security Council. Notice of withdrawal shall include a statement of the extraordinary event or events which a State Party regards as jeopardizing its supreme interests.

ARTICLE X

STATUS OF THE PROTOCOL AND THE ANNEXES

The Annexes to this Treaty, the Protocol, and the Annexes to the Protocol form an integral part of the Treaty. Any reference to this Treaty includes the Annexes to this Treaty, the Protocol and the Annexes to the Protocol.

ARTICLE XI

SIGNATURE

This Treaty shall be open to all States for signature before its entry into force.

ARTICLE XII
RATIFICATION

This Treaty shall be subject to ratification by States Signatories according to their respective constitutional processes.

ARTICLE XIII
ACCESSION

Any State which does not sign this Treaty before its entry into force may accede to it at any time thereafter.

ARTICLE XIV
ENTRY INTO FORCE

1. This Treaty shall enter into force 180 days after the

date of deposit of the instruments of ratification by all States
listed in Annex 2 to this Treaty, but in no case earlier than
two years after its opening for signature.

2. If this Treaty has not entered into force three years
after the date of the anniversary of its opening for signature,
the Depositary shall convene a Conference of the States
that have already deposited their instruments of ratification
upon the request of a majority of those States. That
Conference shall examine the extent to which the
requirement set out in paragraph 1 has been met and shall
consider and decide by consensus what measures
consistent with international law may be undertaken to

accelerate the ratification process in order to facilitate the early entry into force of this Treaty.

3. Unless otherwise decided by the Conference referred to in paragraph 2 or other such conferences, this process shall be repeated at subsequent anniversaries of the opening for signature of this Treaty, until its entry into force.

4. All States Signatories shall be invited to attend the Conference referred to in paragraph 2 and any subsequent conferences as referred to in paragraph 3, as observers.

5. For States whose instruments of ratification or accession are deposited subsequent to the entry into force of this Treaty, it shall enter into force on the 30th day

following the date of deposit of their instruments of
ratification or accession.

ARTICLE XV

RESERVATIONS

The Articles of and the Annexes to this Treaty shall
not be subject to reservations. The provisions of the
Protocol to this Treaty and the Annexes to the Protocol shall
not be subject to reservations incompatible with the object
and purpose of this Treaty.

ARTICLE XVI

DEPOSITARY

1. The Secretary-General of the United Nations shall be
the Depositary of this Treaty and shall receive signatures,
instruments of ratification and instruments of accession.

2. The Depositary shall promptly inform all States Signatories and acceding States of the date of each signature, the date of deposit of each instrument of ratification or accession, the date of the entry into force of this Treaty and of any amendments and changes thereto, and the receipt of other notices.

3. The Depositary shall send duly certified copies of this Treaty to the Governments of the States Signatories and acceding States.

4. This Treaty shall be registered by the Depositary pursuant to Article 102 of the Charter of the United Nations.

ARTICLE XVII

AUTHENTIC TEXTS

This Treaty, of which the Arabic, Chinese, English,
French, Russian and Spanish texts are equally authentic,
shall be deposited with the Secretary-General of the
United Nations.

ANNEX 1 TO THE TREATY

LIST OF STATES PURSUANT TO ARTICLE II, PARAGRAPH 28

Africa

Algeria, Angola, Benin, Botswana, Burkina Faso, Burundi, Cameroon, Cape Verde, Central African Republic, Chad, Comoros, Congo, Côte d'Ivoire, Djibouti, Egypt, Equatorial Guinea, Eritrea, Ethiopia, Gabon, Gambia, Ghana, Guinea, Guinea-Bissau, Kenya, Lesotho, Liberia, Libyan Arab Jamahiriya, Madagascar, Malawi, Mali, Mauritania,

Mauritius, Morocco, Mozambique, Namibia, Niger, Nigeria,
Rwanda, Sao Tome & Principe, Senegal, Seychelles, Sierra
Leone, Somalia, South Africa, Sudan, Swaziland, Togo,
Tunisia, Uganda, United Republic of Tanzania, Zaire,
Zambia, Zimbabwe.

Eastern Europe

Albania, Armenia, Azerbaijan, Belarus, Bosnia and
Herzegovina, Bulgaria, Croatia, Czech Republic, Estonia,
Georgia, Hungary, Latvia, Lithuania, Poland, Republic of
Moldova, Romania, Russian Federation, Slovakia, Slovenia,
-

The former Yugoslav Republic of Macedonia, Ukraine,
Yugoslavia.

Latin America and the Caribbean

Antigua and Barbuda, Argentina, Bahamas, Barbados,
Belize, Bolivia, Brazil, Chile, Colombia, Costa Rica, Cuba,
Dominica, Dominican Republic, Ecuador, El Salvador,
Grenada, Guatemala, Guyana, Haiti, Honduras, Jamaica,
Mexico, Nicaragua, Panama, Paraguay, Peru, Saint Kitts
and Nevis, Saint Lucia, Saint Vincent and the Grenadines,
Suriname, Trinidad and Tobago, Uruguay, Venezuela.

Middle East and South Asia

Afghanistan, Bahrain, Bangladesh, Bhutan, India, Iran (Islamic Republic of), Iraq, Israel, Jordan, Kazakstan, Kuwait, Kyrgyzstan, Lebanon, Maldives, Nepal, Oman, Pakistan, Qatar, Saudi Arabia, Sri Lanka, Syrian Arab Republic, Tajikistan, Turkmenistan, United Arab Emirates, Uzbekistan, Yemen.

North America and Western Europe

Andorra, Austria, Belgium, Canada, Cyprus, Denmark, Finland, France, Germany, Greece, Holy See, Iceland, Ireland, Italy, Liechtenstein, Luxembourg, Malta, Monaco, Netherlands, Norway, Portugal, San Marino, Spain, Sweden, Switzerland, Turkey, United Kingdom of Great

Britain and Northern Ireland, United States of America.

South East Asia, the Pacific and the Far East

Australia, Brunei Darussalam, Cambodia, China, Cook
Islands, Democratic People's Republic of Korea, Fiji,
Indonesia, Japan, Kiribati, Lao People's Democratic
Republic, Malaysia, Marshall Islands, Micronesia (Federated States of), Mongolia, Myanmar, Nauru, New
Zealand, Niue, Palau, Papua New Guinea, Philippines,
Republic of Korea, Samoa, Singapore, Solomon Islands,
Thailand, Tonga, Tuvalu, Vanuatu, Viet Nam.

ANNEX 2 TO THE TREATY

LIST OF STATES PURSUANT TO ARTICLE XIV

List of States members of the Conference on Disarmament as at 18 June 1996 which formally participated in the work of the 1996 session of the

Conference and which appear in Table 1 of the International
Atomic Energy Agency's April 1996 edition of "Nuclear
Power Reactors in the World", and of States members of
the Conference on Disarmament as at 18 June 1996 which
formally participated in the work of the 1996 session of the
Conference and which appear in Table 1 of the International
Atomic Energy Agency's December 1995 edition of "Nuclear
Research Reactors in the World":
Algeria, Argentina, Australia, Austria, Bangladesh, Belgium,
Brazil, Bulgaria, Canada, Chile, China, Colombia, Democratic People's Republic of Korea, Egypt, Finland,
France, Germany, Hungary, India, Indonesia, Iran (Islamic
Republic of), Israel, Italy, Japan, Mexico, Netherlands,

Norway, Pakistan, Peru, Poland, Romania, Republic of
Korea, Russian Federation, Slovakia, South Africa, Spain,
Sweden, Switzerland, Turkey, Ukraine, United Kingdom of
Great Britain and Northern Ireland, United States of
America, Viet Nam, Zaire.

PROTOCOL TO THE COMPREHENSIVE NUCLEAR TEST-BAN TREATY

PART I

THE INTERNATIONAL MONITORING SYSTEM AND
INTERNATIONAL DATA CENTRE FUNCTIONS

A. GENERAL PROVISIONS

1. The International Monitoring System shall comprise
monitoring facilities as set out in Article IV, paragraph 16,
and respective means of communication.

2. The monitoring facilities incorporated into the
International Monitoring System shall consist of those
facilities specified in Annex 1 to this Protocol. The
International Monitoring System shall fulfil the technical and
operational requirements specified in the relevant
operational manuals.

3. The Organization, in accordance with Article II, shall,
in cooperation and consultation with the States Parties, with
other States, and with international organizations as
appropriate, establish and coordinate the operation and
maintenance, and any future agreed modification or
development of the International Monitoring System.

4. In accordance with appropriate agreements or
arrangements and procedures, a State Party or other State
hosting or otherwise taking responsibility for International
Monitoring System facilities and the Technical Secretariat
shall agree and cooperate in establishing, operating,
upgrading, financing, and maintaining monitoring facilities,
related certified laboratories and respective means of
communication within areas under its jurisdiction or control
or elsewhere in conformity with international law. Such
cooperation shall be in accordance with the security and
authentication requirements and technical specifications
contained in the relevant operational manuals. Such a State

shall give the Technical Secretariat authority to access a monitoring facility for checking equipment and communication links, and shall agree to make the necessary changes in the equipment and the operational procedures to meet agreed requirements. The Technical Secretariat shall provide to such States appropriate technical assistance as is deemed by the Executive Council to be required for the proper functioning of the facility as part of the International Monitoring System.

5. Modalities for such cooperation between the Organization and States Parties or States hosting or otherwise taking responsibility for facilities of the International Monitoring System shall be set out in

agreements or arrangements as appropriate in each case.

B. SEISMOLOGICAL MONITORING

6. Each State Party undertakes to cooperate in an international exchange of seismological data to assist in the verification of compliance with this Treaty. This cooperation shall include the establishment and operation of a global network of primary and auxiliary seismological monitoring stations. These stations shall provide data in accordance with agreed procedures to the International Data Centre.

7. The network of primary stations shall consist of the 50 stations specified in Table 1-A of Annex 1 to this Protocol. These stations shall fulfil the technical and operational

requirements specified in the Operational Manual for Seismological Monitoring and the International Exchange of Seismological Data. Uninterrupted data from the primary stations shall be transmitted, directly or through a national data centre, on-line to the International Data Centre.

8. To supplement the primary network, an auxiliary network of 120 stations shall provide information, directly or through a national data centre, to the International Data Centre upon request. The auxiliary stations to be used are listed in Table 1-B of Annex 1 to this Protocol. The auxiliary stations shall fulfil the technical and operational requirements specified in the Operational Manual for

Seismological Monitoring and the International Exchange of
Seismological Data. Data from the auxiliary stations may at
any time be requested by the International Data Centre and
shall be immediately available through on-line computer
connections.

C. RADIONUCLIDE MONITORING

9. Each State Party undertakes to cooperate in an
international exchange of data on radionuclides in the
atmosphere to assist in the verification of compliance with
this Treaty. This cooperation shall include the establishment and operation of a global network of
radionuclide monitoring stations and certified laboratories.
The network shall provide data in accordance with agreed
procedures to the International Data Centre.

10. The network of stations to measure radionuclides in the atmosphere shall comprise an overall network of 80 stations, as specified in Table 2-A of Annex 1 to this Protocol. All stations shall be capable of monitoring for the presence of relevant particulate matter in the atmosphere. Forty of these stations shall also be capable of monitoring for the presence of relevant noble gases upon the entry into force of this Treaty. For this purpose the Conference, at its initial session, shall approve a recommendation by the Preparatory Commission as to which 40 stations from Table 2-A of Annex 1 to this Protocol shall be capable of noble

gas monitoring. At its first regular annual session, the Conference shall consider and decide on a plan for implementing noble gas monitoring capability throughout the network. The Director-General shall prepare a report to the Conference on the modalities for such implementation. All monitoring stations shall fulfil the technical and operational requirements specified in the Operational Manual for Radionuclide Monitoring and the International Exchange of Radionuclide Data.

11. The network of radionuclide monitoring stations shall be supported by laboratories, which shall be certified by the Technical Secretariat in accordance with the relevant

operational manual for the performance, on contract to the
Organization and on a fee-for-service basis, of the analysis

of samples from radionuclide monitoring stations.
Laboratories specified in Table 2-B of Annex 1 to this
Protocol, and appropriately equipped, shall, as required,
also be drawn upon by the Technical Secretariat to perform
additional analysis of samples from radionuclide monitoring
stations. With the agreement of the Executive Council,
further laboratories may be certified by the Technical
Secretariat to perform the routine analysis of samples from
manual monitoring stations where necessary. All certified

laboratories shall provide the results of such analysis to the International Data Centre, and in so doing shall fulfil the technical and operational requirements specified in the Operational Manual on Radionuclide Monitoring and the International Exchange of Radionuclide Data.

D. HYDROACOUSTIC MONITORING

12. Each State Party undertakes to cooperate in an international exchange of hydroacoustic data to assist in the verification of compliance with this Treaty. This cooperation shall include the establishment and operation of a global network of hydroacoustic monitoring stations. These stations shall provide data in accordance with agreed procedures to the International Data Centre.

13. The network of hydroacoustic stations shall consist of
the stations specified in Table 3 of Annex 1 to this Protocol,
and shall comprise an overall network of six hydrophone
and five T-phase stations. These stations shall fulfil the
technical and operational requirements specified in the
Operational Manual for Hydroacoustic Monitoring and the
International Exchange of Hydroacoustic Data.

E. INFRASOUND MONITORING

14. Each State Party undertakes to cooperate in an
international exchange of infrasound data to assist in the
verification of compliance with this Treaty. This cooperation
shall include the establishment and operation of a global
network of infrasound monitoring stations. These stations

shall provide data in accordance with agreed procedures to
the International Data Centre.

15. The network of infrasound stations shall consist of the
stations specified in Table 4 of Annex 1 to this Protocol, and
shall comprise an overall network of 60 stations. These
stations shall fulfil the technical and operational
requirements specified in the Operational Manual for
Infrasound Monitoring and the International Exchange of
Infrasound Data.

F. INTERNATIONAL DATA CENTRE FUNCTIONS

16. The International Data Centre shall receive, collect,
process, analyse, report on and archive data from
International Monitoring System facilities, including the

results of analysis conducted at certified laboratories.

17. The procedures and standard event screening criteria to be used by the International Data Centre in carrying out its agreed functions, in particular for the production of standard reporting products and for the performance of a standard range of services for States Parties, shall be elaborated in the Operational Manual for the International Data Centre and shall be progressively developed. The procedures and criteria developed initially by the Preparatory Commission shall be approved by the Conference at its initial session.

International Data Centre Standard Products

18. The International Data Centre shall apply on a routine

basis automatic processing methods and interactive human analysis to raw International Monitoring System data in order to produce and archive standard International Data Centre products on behalf of all States Parties. These products shall be provided at no cost to States Parties and shall be without prejudice to final judgements with regard to the nature of any event, which shall remain the responsibility of States Parties, and shall include:

(a) Integrated lists of all signals detected by the International Monitoring System, as well as standard event lists and bulletins, including the values and associated uncertainties calculated for each event located by the

International Data Centre, based on a set of standard parameters;

(b) Standard screened event bulletins that result from the application to each event by the International Data Centre of standard event screening criteria, making use of the characterization parameters specified in Annex 2 to this Protocol, with the objective of characterizing, highlighting in the standard event bulletin, and thereby screening out, events considered to be consistent with natural phenomena or non-nuclear, man-made phenomena. The standard event bulletin shall indicate numerically for each event the degree to which that event meets or does not meet the

event screening criteria. In applying standard event
screening, the International Data Centre shall use both
global and supplementary screening criteria to take account
of regional variations where applicable. The International
Data Centre shall progressively enhance its technical
capabilities as experience is gained in the operation of the
International Monitoring System;

(c) Executive summaries, which summarize the data acquired and archived by the International Data Centre, the products of the International Data Centre, and the performance and operational status of the International Monitoring System and International Data Centre; and

(d) Extracts or subsets of the standard International
Data Centre products specified in sub-paragraphs (a) to (c),
selected according to the request of an individual State
Party.

19. The International Data Centre shall carry out, at no
cost to States Parties, special studies to provide in-depth,
technical review by expert analysis of data from the
International Monitoring System, if requested by the
Organization or by a State Party, to improve the estimated
values for the standard signal and event parameters.

International Data Centre Services to States Parties

20. The International Data Centre shall provide States

Parties with open, equal, timely and convenient access to all International Monitoring System data, raw or processed, all International Data Centre products, and all other International Monitoring System data in the archive of the International Data Centre or, through the International Data Centre, of International Monitoring System facilities. The methods for supporting data access and the provision of data shall include the following services:

(a) Automatic and regular forwarding to a State Party of the products of the International Data Centre or the selection by the State Party thereof, and, as requested, the selection by the State Party of International Monitoring System data;

(b) The provision of the data or products generated
in response to ad hoc requests by States Parties for the
retrieval from the International Data Centre and International
Monitoring System facility archives of data and products,
including interactive electronic access to the International
Data Centre database; and

(c) Assisting individual States Parties, at their request and at no cost for reasonable efforts, with expert
technical analysis of International Monitoring System data
and other relevant data provided by the requesting State
Party, in order to help the State Party concerned to identify
the source of specific events. The output of any such

technical analysis shall be considered a product of the
requesting State Party, but shall be available to all States
Parties.

The International Data Centre services specified in subparagraphs
(a) and (b) shall be made available at no cost to each State Party. The volumes and formats of data shall be
set out in the Operational Manual for the International Data
Centre.

National Event Screening

21. The International Data Centre shall, if requested by a
State Party, apply to any of its standard products, on a
regular and automatic basis, national event screening
criteria established by that State Party, and provide the
results of such analysis to that State Party. This service

shall be undertaken at no cost to the requesting State Party.

The output of such national event screening processes shall be considered a product of the requesting State Party.

Technical Assistance

22. The International Data Centre shall, where required, provide technical assistance to individual States Parties:

(a) In formulating their requirements for selection and screening of data and products;

(b) By installing at the International Data Centre, at no cost to a requesting State Party for reasonable efforts, computer algorithms or software provided by that State Party to compute new signal and event parameters that are

not included in the Operational Manual for the International
Data Centre, the output being considered products of the
requesting State Party; and

(c) By assisting States Parties to develop the capability to receive, process and analyse International
Monitoring System data at a national data centre.

23. The International Data Centre shall continuously
monitor and report on the operational status of the
International Monitoring System facilities, of communications links, and of its own processing systems.
It shall provide immediate notification to those responsible
should the operational performance of any component fail to
meet agreed levels set out in the relevant operational

manual.

PART II
ON-SITE INSPECTIONS
A. GENERAL PROVISIONS

1. The procedures in this Part shall be implemented pursuant to the provisions for on-site inspections set out in Article IV.

2. The on-site inspection shall be carried out in the area where the event that triggered the on-site inspection request occurred.

3. The area of an on-site inspection shall be continuous and its size shall not exceed 1,000 square kilometres. There shall be no linear distance greater than 50 kilometres in any direction.

4. The duration of an on-site inspection shall not exceed

60 days from the date of the approval of the on-site inspection request in accordance with Article IV, paragraph 46, but may be extended by a maximum of 70 days in accordance with Article IV, paragraph 49.

5. If the inspection area specified in the inspection mandate extends to the territory or other place under the jurisdiction or control of more than one State Party, the provisions on on-site inspections shall, as appropriate, apply to each of the States Parties to which the inspection area extends.

6. In cases where the inspection area is under the jurisdiction or control of the inspected State Party but is

located on the territory of another State Party or where the access from the point of entry to the inspection area requires transit through the territory of a State Party other than the inspected State Party, the inspected State Party shall exercise the rights and fulfil the obligations concerning such inspections in accordance with this Protocol. In such a case, the State Party on whose territory the inspection area is located shall facilitate the inspection and shall provide for the necessary support to enable the inspection team to carry out its tasks in a timely and effective manner. States Parties through whose territory transit is required to reach the inspection area shall facilitate such transit.

7. In cases where the inspection area is under the jurisdiction or control of the inspected State Party but is located on the territory of a State not Party to this Treaty, the inspected State Party shall take all necessary measures to ensure that the inspection can be carried out in accordance with this Protocol. A State Party that has under its jurisdiction or control one or more areas on the territory of a State not Party to this Treaty shall take all necessary measures to ensure acceptance by the State on whose territory the inspection area is located of inspectors and inspection assistants designated to that State Party. If an

inspected State Party is unable to ensure access, it shall demonstrate that it took all necessary measures to ensure access.

8. In cases where the inspection area is located on the territory of a State Party but is under the jurisdiction or control of a State not Party to this Treaty, the State Party shall take all necessary measures required of an inspected State Party and a State Party on whose territory the inspection area is located, without prejudice to the rules and practices of international law, to ensure that the on-site inspection can be carried out in accordance with this Protocol. If the State Party is unable to ensure access to

the inspection area, it shall demonstrate that it took all
necessary measures to ensure access, without prejudice to
the rules and practices of international law.

9. The size of the inspection team shall be kept to the
minimum necessary for the proper fulfilment of the
inspection mandate. The total number of members of the
inspection team present on the territory of the inspected
State Party at any given time, except during the conduct of
drilling, shall not exceed 40 persons. No national of the
requesting State Party or the inspected State Party shall be
a member of the inspection team.

10. The Director-General shall determine the size of the

inspection team and select its members from the list of inspectors and inspection assistants, taking into account the circumstances of a particular request.

11. The inspected State Party shall provide for or arrange the amenities necessary for the inspection team, such as communication means, interpretation services, transportation, working space, lodging, meals, and medical care.

12. The inspected State Party shall be reimbursed by the Organization, in a reasonably short period of time after conclusion of the inspection, for all expenses, including those mentioned in paragraphs 11 and 49, related to the stay and functional activities of the inspection team on the

territory of the inspected State Party.

13. Procedures for the implementation of on-site inspections shall be detailed in the Operational Manual for On-Site Inspections.

B. STANDING ARRANGEMENTS

Designation of Inspectors and Inspection Assistants

14. An inspection team may consist of inspectors and inspection assistants. An on-site inspection shall only be carried out by qualified inspectors specially designated for this function. They may be assisted by specially designated inspection assistants, such as technical and administrative personnel, aircrew and interpreters.

15. Inspectors and inspection assistants shall be nominated for designation by the States Parties or, in the

case of staff of the Technical Secretariat, by the Director-General, on the basis of their expertise and experience relevant to the purpose and functions of on-site inspections. The nominees shall be approved in advance by the States Parties in accordance with paragraph 18.

16. Each State Party, no later than 30 days after the entry into force of this Treaty for it, shall notify the Director-General of the names, dates of birth, sex, ranks, qualifications and professional experience of the persons proposed by the State Party for designation as inspectors and inspection assistants.

17. No later than 60 days after the entry into force of this Treaty, the Technical Secretariat shall communicate in

writing to all States Parties an initial list of the names,
nationalities, dates of birth, sex and ranks of the inspectors
and inspection assistants proposed for designation by the
Director-General and the States Parties, as well as a
description of their qualifications and professional
experience.

18. Each State Party shall immediately acknowledge
receipt of the initial list of inspectors and inspection
assistants proposed for designation. Any inspector or
inspection assistant included in this list shall be regarded as
accepted unless a State Party, no later than 30 days after
acknowledgment of receipt of the list, declares its

non-acceptance in writing. The State Party may include the
reason for the objection. In the case of non-acceptance, the
proposed inspector or inspection assistant shall not

-114-

undertake or participate in on-site inspection activities on
the territory or in any other place under the jurisdiction or
control of the State Party that has declared its non-acceptance. The Technical Secretariat shall immediately confirm receipt of the notification of objection.

19. Whenever additions or changes to the list of inspectors and inspection assistants are proposed by the Director-General or a State Party, replacement inspectors
and inspection assistants shall be designated in the same
manner as set forth with respect to the initial list. Each

State Party shall promptly notify the Technical Secretariat if an inspector or inspection assistant nominated by it can no longer fulfil the duties of an inspector or inspection assistant.

20. The Technical Secretariat shall keep the list of inspectors and inspection assistants up to date and notify all States Parties of any additions or changes to the list.

21. A State Party requesting an on-site inspection may propose that an inspector from the list of inspectors and inspection assistants serve as its observer in accordance with Article IV, paragraph 61.

22. Subject to paragraph 23, a State Party shall have the

right at any time to object to an inspector or inspection assistant who has already been accepted. It shall notify the Technical Secretariat of its objection in writing and may include the reason for the objection. Such objection shall come into effect 30 days after receipt of the notification by the Technical Secretariat. The Technical Secretariat shall immediately confirm receipt of the notification of the objection and inform the objecting and nominating States Parties of the date on which the inspector or inspection assistant shall cease to be designated for that State Party.

23. A State Party that has been notified of an inspection shall not seek the removal from the inspection team of any

of the inspectors or inspection assistants named in the
inspection mandate.

24. The number of inspectors and inspection assistants
accepted by a State Party must be sufficient to allow for
availability of appropriate numbers of inspectors and
inspection assistants. If, in the opinion of the
Director-General, the non-acceptance by a State Party of
proposed inspectors or inspection assistants impedes the
designation of a sufficient number of inspectors and
inspection assistants or otherwise hampers the effective
fulfilment of the purposes of an on-site inspection, the
Director-General shall refer the issue to the Executive Council.

25. Each inspector included in the list of inspectors and inspection assistants shall receive relevant training. Such training shall be provided by the Technical Secretariat pursuant to the procedures specified in the Operational Manual for On-Site Inspections. The Technical Secretariat shall co-ordinate, in agreement with the States Parties, a schedule of training for the inspectors.

Privileges and Immunities

26. Following acceptance of the initial list of inspectors and inspection assistants as provided for in paragraph 18 or as subsequently altered in accordance with paragraph 19, each State Party shall be obliged to issue, in accordance with its national procedures and upon application by an

inspector or inspection assistant, multiple entry/exit and/or
transit visas and other relevant documents to enable each
inspector and inspection assistant to enter and to remain on
the territory of that State Party for the sole purpose of
carrying out inspection activities. Each State Party shall
issue the necessary visa or travel documents for this
purpose no later than 48 hours after receipt of the
application or immediately upon arrival of the inspection
team at the point of entry on the territory of the State Party.
Such documents shall be valid for as long as is necessary
to enable the inspector or inspection assistant to remain on

the territory of the inspected State Party for the sole purpose of carrying out the inspection activities.

27. To exercise their functions effectively, members of the inspection team shall be accorded privileges and immunities as set forth in sub-paragraphs (a) to (i). Privileges and immunities shall be granted to members of the inspection team for the sake of this Treaty and not for the personal benefit of the individuals themselves. Such privileges and immunities shall be accorded to them for the entire period between arrival on and departure from the territory of the inspected State Party, and thereafter with respect to acts previously performed in the exercise of their official functions.

(a) The members of the inspection team shall be accorded the inviolability enjoyed by diplomatic agents pursuant to Article 29 of the Vienna Convention on Diplomatic Relations of 18 April 1961;

(b) The living quarters and office premises occupied by the inspection team carrying out inspection activities pursuant to this Treaty shall be accorded the inviolability and protection accorded to the premises of diplomatic agents pursuant to Article 30, paragraph 1, of the Vienna Convention on Diplomatic Relations;

(c) The papers and correspondence, including records, of the inspection team shall enjoy the inviolability accorded to all papers and correspondence of diplomatic agents pursuant to Article 30, paragraph 2, of the Vienna Convention on Diplomatic Relations. The inspection team shall have the right to use codes for their communications with the Technical Secretariat;

(d) Samples and approved equipment carried by members of the inspection team shall be inviolable subject to provisions contained in this Treaty and exempt from all customs duties. Hazardous samples shall be transported in accordance with relevant regulations;

(e) The members of the inspection team shall be accorded the immunities accorded to diplomatic agents pursuant to Article 31, paragraphs 1, 2 and 3, of the Vienna Convention on Diplomatic Relations;

(f) The members of the inspection team carrying out prescribed activities pursuant to this Treaty shall be accorded the exemption from dues and taxes accorded to diplomatic agents pursuant to Article 34 of the Vienna Convention on Diplomatic Relations;

(g) The members of the inspection team shall be permitted to bring into the territory of the inspected State Party, without payment of any customs duties or related charges, articles for personal use, with the exception of articles the import or export of which is prohibited by law or controlled by quarantine regulations;

(h) The members of the inspection team shall be accorded the same currency and exchange facilities as are accorded to representatives of foreign Governments on temporary official missions; and

(i) The members of the inspection team shall not engage in any professional or commercial activity for personal profit on the territory of the inspected State Party.

28. When transiting the territory of States Parties other than the inspected State Party, the members of the inspection team shall be accorded the privileges and immunities enjoyed by diplomatic agents pursuant to Article 40, paragraph 1, of the Vienna Convention on Diplomatic Relations. Papers and correspondence, including records, and samples and approved equipment carried by them,

shall be accorded the privileges and immunities set forth in
paragraph 27 (c) and (d).

29. Without prejudice to their privileges and immunities
the members of the inspection team shall be obliged to
respect the laws and regulations of the inspected State
Party and, to the extent that is consistent with the inspection
mandate, shall be obliged not to interfere in the internal
affairs of that State. If the inspected State Party considers
that there has been an abuse of privileges and immunities
specified in this Protocol, consultations shall be held
between the State Party and the Director-General to
determine whether such an abuse has occurred and, if so

determined, to prevent a repetition of such an abuse.

30. The immunity from jurisdiction of members of the inspection team may be waived by the Director-General in those cases when the Director-General is of the opinion that immunity would impede the course of justice and that it can be waived without prejudice to the implementation of the provisions of this Treaty. Waiver must always be express.

31. Observers shall be accorded the same privileges and immunities accorded to members of the inspection team pursuant to this section, except for those accorded pursuant to paragraph 27 (d).

Points of Entry

32. Each State Party shall designate its points of entry and shall supply the required information to the Technical Secretariat no later than 30 days after this Treaty enters into force for it. These points of entry shall be such that the inspection team can reach any inspection area from at least one point of entry within 24 hours. Locations of points of entry shall be provided to all States Parties by the Technical Secretariat. Points of entry may also serve as points of exit.

33. Each State Party may change its points of entry by giving notice of such change to the Technical Secretariat. Changes shall become effective 30 days after the Technical Secretariat receives such notification, to allow appropriate

notification to all States Parties.

34. If the Technical Secretariat considers that there are insufficient points of entry for the timely conduct of inspections or that changes to the points of entry proposed by a State Party would hamper such timely conduct of inspections, it shall enter into consultations with the State Party concerned to resolve the problem.

Arrangements for Use of Non-Scheduled Aircraft

35. Where timely travel to the point of entry is not feasible using scheduled commercial flights, an inspection team may utilize non-scheduled aircraft. No later than 30 days after this Treaty enters into force for it, each State Party shall

inform the Technical Secretariat of the standing diplomatic
clearance number for non-scheduled aircraft transporting an
inspection team and equipment necessary for inspection.
Aircraft routings shall be along established international
airways that are agreed upon between the State Party and
the Technical Secretariat as the basis for such diplomatic
clearance.

Approved Inspection Equipment

36. The Conference, at its initial session, shall consider
and approve a list of equipment for use during on-site
inspections. Each State Party may submit proposals for the
inclusion of equipment in the list. Specifications for the use
of the equipment, as detailed in the Operational Manual for

On-Site Inspections, shall take account of safety and confidentiality considerations where such equipment is likely to be used.

37. The equipment for use during on-site inspections shall consist of core equipment for the inspection activities and techniques specified in paragraph 69 and auxiliary equipment necessary for the effective and timely conduct of on-site inspections.

38. The Technical Secretariat shall ensure that all types of approved equipment are available for on-site inspections when required. When required for an on-site inspection, the Technical Secretariat shall duly certify that the equipment

has been calibrated, maintained and protected. To facilitate
the checking of the equipment at the point of entry by the
inspected State Party, the Technical Secretariat shall
provide documentation and attach seals to authenticate the
certification.

39. Any permanently held equipment shall be in the
custody of the Technical Secretariat. The Technical
Secretariat shall be responsible for the maintenance and
calibration of such equipment.

40. As appropriate, the Technical Secretariat shall make
arrangements with States Parties to provide equipment
mentioned in the list. Such States Parties shall be

responsible for the maintenance and calibration of such equipment.

C. ON-SITE INSPECTION REQUEST, INSPECTION MANDATE AND NOTIFICATION OF INSPECTION

On-Site Inspection Request

41. Pursuant to Article IV, paragraph 37, the on-site inspection request shall contain at least the following information:

(a) The estimated geographical and vertical coordinates of the location of the event that triggered the request with an indication of the possible margin of error;

(b) The proposed boundaries of the area to be inspected, specified on a map and in accordance with paragraphs 2 and 3;

(c) The State Party or States Parties to be

inspected or an indication that the area to be inspected or
part thereof is beyond the jurisdiction or control of any State;
(d) The probable environment of the event that triggered the request;
(e) The estimated time of the event that triggered
the request, with an indication of the possible margin of
error;
(f) All data upon which the request is based;
(g) The personal details of the proposed observer, if
any; and
(h) The results of a consultation and clarification process in accordance with Article IV, or an explanation, if
relevant, of the reasons why such a consultation and
clarification process has not been carried out.

Inspection Mandate

42. The mandate for an on-site inspection shall contain:

(a) The decision of the Executive Council on the onsite
inspection request;

(b) The name of the State Party or States Parties to
be inspected or an indication that the inspection area or part
thereof is beyond the jurisdiction or control of any State;

(c) The location and boundaries of the inspection
area specified on a map, taking into account all information
on which the request was based and all other available
technical information, in consultation with the requesting
State Party;

(d) The planned types of activity of the inspection
team in the inspection area;

(e) The point of entry to be used by the inspection

team;
(f) Any transit or basing points, as appropriate;
(g) The name of the head of the inspection team;
(h) The names of members of the inspection team;
(i) The name of the proposed observer, if any; and
(j) The list of equipment to be used in the inspection area.

If a decision by the Executive Council pursuant to Article IV, paragraphs 46 to 49, necessitates a modification of the inspection mandate, the Director-General may update the mandate with respect to sub-paragraphs (d), (h) and (j), as appropriate. The Director-General shall immediately notify the inspected State Party of any such modification.

Notification of Inspection

43. The notification made by the Director-General
pursuant to Article IV, paragraph 55 shall include the
following information:
(a) The inspection mandate;
(b) The date and estimated time of arrival of the inspection team at the point of entry;
(c) The means of arrival at the point of entry;
(d) If appropriate, the standing diplomatic clearance
number for non-scheduled aircraft; and

(e) A list of any equipment which the Director-General requests the inspected State Party to
make available to the inspection team for use in the
inspection area.

44. The inspected State Party shall acknowledge receipt
of the notification by the Director-General no later than 12
hours after having received the notification.

D. PRE-INSPECTION ACTIVITIES

Entry Into the Territory of the Inspected State Party, Activities at the Point of Entry and Transfer to the Inspection Area

45. The inspected State Party that has been notified of
the arrival of the inspection team shall ensure the immediate
entry of the inspection team into its territory.

46. When a non-scheduled aircraft is used for travel to
the point of entry, the Technical Secretariat shall provide the
inspected State Party with a flight plan, through the National
Authority, for the flight of the aircraft from the last airfield
prior to entering the airspace of that State Party to the point
of entry, no less than six hours before the scheduled

departure time from that airfield. Such a plan shall be filed in accordance with the procedures of the International Civil Aviation Organization applicable to civil aircraft. The Technical Secretariat shall include in the remarks section of the flight plan the standing diplomatic clearance number and the appropriate notation identifying the aircraft as an inspection aircraft. If a military aircraft is used, the Technical Secretariat shall request prior authorization from the inspected State Party to enter its airspace.

47. No less than three hours before the scheduled departure of the inspection team from the last airfield prior to entering the airspace of the inspected State Party, the

inspected State Party shall ensure that the flight plan filed in accordance with paragraph 46 is approved, so that the inspection team may arrive at the point of entry by the estimated arrival time.

48. Where necessary, the head of the inspection team and the representative of the inspected State Party shall agree on a basing point and a flight plan from the point of entry to the basing point and, if necessary, to the inspection area.

49. The inspected State Party shall provide for or arrange parking, security protection, servicing and fuel as required by the Technical Secretariat for the aircraft of the inspection

team at the point of entry and, where necessary, at the basing point and at the inspection area. Such aircraft shall not be liable for landing fees, departure tax, and similar charges. This paragraph shall also apply to aircraft used for overflight during the on-site inspection.

50. Subject to paragraph 51, there shall be no restriction by the inspected State Party on the inspection team bringing approved equipment that is in conformity with the inspection mandate into the territory of that State Party, or on its use in accordance with the provisions of the Treaty and this Protocol.

51. The inspected State Party shall have the right, without prejudice to the time-frame specified in paragraph

54, to check in the presence of inspection team members at
the point of entry that the equipment has been approved
and certified in accordance with paragraph 38. The
inspected State Party may exclude equipment that is not in
conformity with the inspection mandate or that has not been
approved and certified in accordance with paragraph 38.

52. Immediately upon arrival at the point of entry and
without prejudice to the time-frame specified in paragraph
54, the head of the inspection team shall present to the
representative of the inspected State Party

54, the head of the inspection team shall present to the representative of the inspected State Party the inspection mandate and an initial inspection plan prepared by the inspection team specifying the activities to be carried out by it. The inspection team shall be briefed by representatives of the inspected State Party with the aid of maps and other documentation as appropriate. The briefing shall include relevant natural terrain features, safety and confidentiality issues, and logistical arrangements for the inspection. The

inspected State Party may indicate locations within the
inspection area that, in its view, are not related to the
purpose of the inspection.

53. After the pre-inspection briefing, the inspection team
shall, as appropriate, modify the initial inspection plan,
taking into account any comments by the inspected State
Party. The modified inspection plan shall be made available
to the representative of the inspected State Party.

54. The inspected State Party shall do everything in its
power to provide assistance and to ensure the safe conduct
of the inspection team, the approved equipment specified in
paragraphs 50 and 51 and baggage from the point of entry

to the inspection area no later than 36 hours after arrival at

the point of entry, if no other timing has been agreed upon within the time-frame specified in paragraph 57.

55. To confirm that the area to which the inspection team has been transported corresponds to the inspection area specified in the inspection mandate, the inspection team shall have the right to use approved location-finding equipment. The inspected State Party shall assist the inspection team in this task.

E. CONDUCT OF INSPECTIONS

General Rules

56. The inspection team shall discharge its functions in accordance with the provisions of the Treaty and this

Protocol.

57. The inspection team shall begin its inspection activities in the inspection area as soon as possible, but in no case later than 72 hours after arrival at the point of entry.

58. The activities of the inspection team shall be so arranged as to ensure the timely and effective discharge of its functions and the least possible inconvenience to the inspected State Party and disturbance to the inspection area.

59. In cases where the inspected State Party has been requested, pursuant to paragraph 43 (e) or in the course of the inspection, to make available any equipment for use by

the inspection team in the inspection area, the inspected
State Party shall comply with the request to the extent it
can.

60. During the on-site inspection the inspection team
shall have, inter alia:

(a) The right to determine how the inspection will
proceed, consistent with the inspection mandate and taking
into account any steps taken by the inspected State Party
consistent with the provisions on managed access;

(b) The right to modify the inspection plan, as necessary, to ensure the effective execution of the
inspection;

(c) The obligation to take into account the recommendations and suggested modifications by the
inspected State Party to the inspection plan;

(d) The right to request clarifications in connection with ambiguities that may arise during the inspection;

(e) The obligation to use only those techniques specified in paragraph 69 and to refrain from activities that are not relevant to the purpose of the inspection. The team shall collect and document such facts as are related to the purpose of the inspection, but shall neither seek nor document information that is clearly unrelated thereto. Any material collected and subsequently found not to be relevant shall be returned to the inspected State Party;

(f) The obligation to take into account and include in its report data and explanations on the nature of the event that triggered the request, provided by the inspected State Party from the national monitoring networks of the inspected State Party and from other sources;

(g) The obligation to provide the inspected State Party, at its request, with copies of the information and data collected in the inspection area; and

(h) The obligation to respect the confidentiality and the safety and health regulations of the inspected State Party.

61. During the on-site inspection the inspected State Party shall have, inter alia:

(a) The right to make recommendations at any time to the inspection team regarding possible modification of the inspection plan;

(b) The right and the obligation to provide a

representative to liaise with the inspection team;

(c) The right to have representatives accompany the inspection team during the performance of its duties and
observe all inspection activities carried out by the inspection
team. This shall not delay or otherwise hinder the
inspection team in the exercise of its functions;

(d) The right to provide additional information and to
request the collection and documentation of additional facts
it believes are relevant to the inspection;

(e) The right to examine all photographic and measurement products as well as samples and to retain any
photographs or parts thereof showing sensitive sites not
related to the purpose of the inspection. The inspected
State Party shall have the right to receive duplicate copies

of all photographic and measurement products. The inspected State Party shall have the right to retain photographic originals and first-generation photographic products and to put photographs or parts thereof under joint seal within its territory. The inspected State Party shall have the right to provide its own camera operator to take still/video photographs as requested by the inspection team. Otherwise, these functions shall be performed by members of the inspection team;

(f) The right to provide the inspection team, from its national monitoring networks and from other sources, with data and explanations on the nature of the event that triggered the request; and

(g) The obligation to provide the inspection team with such clarification as may be necessary to resolve any ambiguities that arise during the inspection.

Communications

62. The members of the inspection team shall have the right at all times during the on-site inspection to communicate with each other and with the Technical Secretariat. For this purpose they may use their own duly approved and certified equipment with the consent of the inspected State Party, to the extent that the inspected State Party does not provide them with access to other telecommunications.

Observer

63. In accordance with Article IV, paragraph 61, the requesting State Party shall liaise with the Technical Secretariat to co-ordinate the arrival of the observer at the same point of entry or basing point as the inspection team within a reasonable period of the arrival of the inspection team.

64. The observer shall have the right throughout the inspection to be in communication with the embassy of the requesting State Party located in the inspected State Party or, in the case of absence of an embassy, with the requesting State Party itself.

65. The observer shall have the right to arrive at the inspection area and to have access to and within the

inspection area as granted by the inspected State Party.

66. The observer shall have the right to make recommendations to the inspection team throughout the inspection.

67. Throughout the inspection, the inspection team shall keep the observer informed about the conduct of the inspection and the findings.

68. Throughout the inspection, the inspected State Party shall provide or arrange for the amenities necessary for the observer similar to those enjoyed by the inspection team as described in paragraph 11. All costs in connection with the stay of the observer on the territory of the inspected State Party shall be borne by the requesting State Party.

Inspection Activities and Techniques

69. The following inspection activities may be conducted
and techniques used, in accordance with the provisions on
managed access, on collection, handling and analysis of
samples, and on overflights:

(a) Position finding from the air and at the surface to
confirm the boundaries of the inspection area and establish
co-ordinates of locations therein, in support of the inspection
activities;

(b) Visual observation, video and still photography
and multi-spectral imaging, including infrared
measurements, at and below the surface, and
from the air,
to search for anomalies or artifacts;

(c) Measurement of levels of radioactivity above, at

and below the surface, using gamma radiation monitoring
and energy resolution analysis from the air, and at or under
the surface, to search for and identify radiation anomalies;

(d) Environmental sampling and analysis of solids,
liquids and gases from above, at and below the surface to
detect anomalies;

(e) Passive seismological monitoring for aftershocks to localize the search area and facilitate
determination of the nature of an event;

(f) Resonance seismometry and active seismic surveys to search for and locate underground anomalies,
including cavities and rubble zones;

(g) Magnetic and gravitational field mapping, ground
penetrating radar and electrical conductivity measurements

at the surface and from the air, as appropriate, to detect anomalies or artifacts; and

(h) Drilling to obtain radioactive samples.

70. Up to 25 days after the approval of the on-site inspection in accordance with Article IV, paragraph 46, the inspection team shall have the right to conduct any of the activities and use any of the techniques listed in paragraph 69 (a) to (e). Following the approval of the continuation of the inspection in accordance with Article IV, paragraph 47, the inspection team shall have the right to conduct any of the activities and use any of the techniques listed in paragraph 69 (a) to (g). The inspection team shall only

conduct drilling after the approval of the Executive Council
in accordance with Article IV, paragraph 48. If the
inspection team requests an extension of the inspection
duration in accordance with Article IV, paragraph 49, it shall
indicate in its request which of the activities and techniques
listed in paragraph 69 it intends to carry out in order to be
able to fulfil its mandate.

Overflights

71. The inspection team shall have the right to conduct
an overflight over the inspection area during the on-site
inspection for the purposes of providing the inspection team
with a general orientation of the inspection area, narrowing

down and optimizing the locations for ground-based
inspection and facilitating the collection of factual evidence,
using equipment specified in paragraph 79.

72. The overflight shall be conducted as soon as practically possible. The total duration of the overflight over
the inspection area shall be no more than 12 hours.

73. Additional overflights using equipment specified in
paragraphs 79 and 80 may be conducted subject to the
agreement of the inspected State Party.

74. The area to be covered by overflights shall not extend
beyond the inspection area.

75. The inspected State Party shall have the right to
impose restrictions or, in exceptional cases and with
reasonable justification, prohibitions on the overflight of

sensitive sites not related to the purpose of the inspection.
Restrictions may relate to the flight altitude, the number of
passes and circling, the duration of hovering, the type of
aircraft, the number of inspectors on board, and the type of
measurements or observations. If the inspection team
considers that the restrictions or prohibitions on the
overflight of sensitive sites may impede the fulfilment of its
mandate, the inspected State Party shall make every
reasonable effort to provide alternative means of inspection.

76. Overflights shall be conducted according to a flight
plan duly filed and approved in accordance with aviation

rules and regulations of the inspected State Party. Flight safety regulations of the inspected State Party shall be strictly observed throughout all flying operations.

77. During overflights landing should normally be authorized only for purposes of staging or refuelling.

78. Overflights shall be conducted at altitudes as requested by the inspection team consistent with the activities to be conducted, visibility conditions, as well as the aviation and the safety regulations of the inspected State Party and its right to protect sensitive information not related to the purposes of the inspection. Overflights shall be conducted up to a maximum altitude of 1,500 metres above

the surface.

79. For the overflight conducted pursuant to paragraphs
71 and 72, the following equipment may be used on board
the aircraft:

-143-

(a) Field glasses;
(b) Passive location-finding equipment;
(c) Video cameras; and
(d) Hand-held still cameras.

80. For any additional overflights conducted pursuant to
paragraph 73, inspectors on board the aircraft may also use
portable, easily installed equipment for:
(a) Multi-spectral (including infrared) imagery;
(b) Gamma spectroscopy; and
(c) Magnetic field mapping.

81. Overflights shall be conducted with a relatively slow
fixed or rotary wing aircraft. The aircraft shall afford a
broad, unobstructed view of the surface below.

82. The inspected State Party shall have the right to provide its own aircraft, pre-equipped as appropriate in accordance with the technical requirements of the relevant

-144-

operational manual, and crew. Otherwise, the aircraft shall be provided or rented by the Technical Secretariat.

83. If the aircraft is provided or rented by the Technical Secretariat, the inspected State Party shall have the right to check the aircraft to ensure that it is equipped with approved inspection equipment. Such checking shall be completed within the time-frame specified in paragraph 57.

84. Personnel on board the aircraft shall consist of:

(a) The minimum number of flight crew consistent
with the safe operation of the aircraft;
(b) Up to four members of the inspection team;
(c) Up to two representatives of the inspected State
Party;
(d) An observer, if any, subject to the agreement of
the inspected State Party; and
(e) An interpreter, if necessary.
85. Procedures for the implementation of overflights shall
be detailed in the Operational Manual for On-Site
Inspections.

Managed Access

86. The inspection team shall have the right to access the
inspection area in accordance with the provisions of the
Treaty and this Protocol.

87. The inspected State Party shall provide access within the inspection area in accordance with the time-frame specified in paragraph 57.

88. Pursuant to Article IV, paragraph 57 and paragraph 86 above, the rights and obligations of the inspected State Party shall include:

(a) The right to take measures to protect sensitive installations and locations in accordance with this Protocol;

(b) The obligation, when access is restricted within the inspection area, to make every reasonable effort to satisfy the requirements of the inspection mandate through alternative means. Resolving any questions regarding one or more aspects of the inspection shall not delay or interfere with the conduct of the inspection team of other aspects of the inspection; and

(c) The right to make the final decision regarding any access of the inspection team, taking into account its obligations under this Treaty and the provisions on managed access.

89. Pursuant to Article IV, paragraph 57 (b) and paragraph 88 (a) above, the inspected State Party shall have the right throughout the inspection area to take measures to protect sensitive installations and locations and to prevent disclosure of confidential information not related to the purpose of the inspection. Such measures may include, inter alia:

(a) Shrouding of sensitive displays, stores, and

equipment;
(b) Restricting measurements of radionuclide activity and nuclear radiation to determining the presence or
absence of those types and energies of radiation relevant to
the purpose of the inspection;
(c) Restricting the taking of or analysing of samples
to determining the presence or absence of radioactive or

-147-

other products relevant to the purpose of the inspection;
(d) Managing access to buildings and other structures in accordance with paragraphs 90 and 91; and
(e) Declaring restricted-access sites in accordance
with paragraphs 92 to 96.
90. Access to buildings and other structures shall be
deferred until after the approval of the continuation of the

on-site inspection in accordance with Article IV, paragraph
47, except for access to buildings and other structures
housing the entrance to a mine, other excavations, or
caverns of large volume not otherwise accessible. For such
buildings and structures, the inspection team shall have the
right only of transit, as directed by the inspected State
Party, in order to enter such mines, caverns or other
excavations.

91. If, following the approval of the continuation of the
inspection in accordance with Article IV, paragraph 47, the
inspection team demonstrates credibly to the inspected
State Party that access to buildings and other structures is

necessary to fulfil the inspection mandate and that the necessary activities authorized in the mandate could not be carried out from the outside, the inspection team shall have the right to gain access to such buildings or other structures. The head of the inspection team shall request access to a specific building or structure indicating the purpose of such access, the specific number of inspectors, as well as the intended activities. The modalities for access shall be subject to negotiation between the inspection team and the inspected State Party. The inspected State Party shall have the right to impose restrictions or, in exceptional cases and with reasonable justification, prohibitions, on the access to buildings and other structures.

92. When restricted-access sites are declared pursuant to paragraph 89 (e), each such site shall be no larger than 4 square kilometres. The inspected State Party has the right to declare up to 50 square kilometres of restrictedaccess sites. If more than one restricted-access site is declared, each such site shall be separated from any other such site by a minimum distance of 20 metres. Each restricted-access site shall have clearly defined and accessible boundaries.

93. The size, location, and boundaries of restrictedaccess sites shall be presented to the head of the inspection team no later than the time that the inspection

team seeks access to a location that contains all or part of such a site.

94. The inspection team shall have the right to place equipment and take other steps necessary to conduct its inspection up to the boundary of a restricted-access site.

95. The inspection team shall be permitted to observe visually all open places within the restricted-access site from the boundary of the site.

96. The inspection team shall make every reasonable effort to fulfil the inspection mandate outside the declared restricted-access sites prior to requesting access to such sites. If at any time the inspection team demonstrates

credibly to the inspected State Party that the necessary activities authorized in the mandate could not be carried out from the outside and that access to a restricted-access site is necessary to fulfil the mandate, some members of the inspection team shall be granted access to accomplish specific tasks within the site. The inspected State Party shall have the right to shroud or otherwise protect sensitive equipment, objects and materials not related to the purpose of the inspection. The number of inspectors shall be kept to the minimum necessary to complete the tasks related to the inspection. The modalities for such access shall be subject

to negotiation between the inspection team and the
inspected State Party.

Collection, Handling and Analysis of Samples

97. Subject to paragraphs 86 to 96 and 98 to 100, the
inspection team shall have the right to collect and remove
relevant samples from the inspection area.

98. Whenever possible, the inspection team shall analyse
samples on-site. Representatives of the inspected State
Party shall have the right to be present when samples are
analysed on-site. At the request of the inspection team, the
inspected State Party shall, in accordance with agreed
procedures, provide assistance for the analysis of samples
on-site. The inspection team shall have the right to transfer

samples for off-site analysis at laboratories designated by the Organization only if it demonstrates that the necessary sample analysis cannot be performed on-site.

99. The inspected State Party shall have the right to retain portions of all samples collected when these samples are analysed and may take duplicate samples.

100. The inspected State Party shall have the right to request that any unused samples or portions thereof be returned.

101. The designated laboratories shall conduct chemical and physical analysis of the samples transferred for off-site analysis. Details of such analysis shall be elaborated in the Operational Manual for On-Site Inspections.

102. The Director-General shall have the primary responsibility for the security, integrity and preservation of samples and for ensuring that the confidentiality of samples transferred for off-site analysis is protected. The Director-General shall do so in accordance with procedures contained in the Operational Manual for On-Site Inspections. The Director-General shall, in any case:

(a) Establish a stringent regime governing the collection, handling, transport and analysis of samples;

(b) Certify the laboratories designated to perform different types of analysis;

(c) Oversee the standardization of equipment and procedures at these designated laboratories and of mobile analytical equipment and procedures;

(d) Monitor quality control and overall standards in relation to the certification of these laboratories and in relation to mobile equipment and procedures; and

(e) Select from among the designated laboratories those which shall perform analytical or other functions in relation to specific investigations.

103. When off-site analysis is to be performed, samples shall be analysed in at least two designated laboratories. The Technical Secretariat shall ensure the expeditious processing of the analysis. The samples shall be accounted for by the Technical Secretariat and any unused samples or portions thereof shall be returned to the Technical Secretariat.

104. The Technical Secretariat shall compile the results of the laboratory analysis of samples relevant to the purpose of the inspection. Pursuant to Article IV, paragraph 63, the Director-General shall transmit any such results promptly to the inspected State Party for comments and thereafter to the Executive Council and to all other States Parties and shall include detailed information concerning the equipment and methodology employed by the designated laboratories.

Conduct of Inspections in Areas beyond the Jurisdiction or Control of any State

105. In case of an on-site inspection in an area beyond the jurisdiction or control of any State, the Director-General

shall consult with the appropriate States Parties and agree
on any transit or basing points to facilitate a speedy arrival
of the inspection team in the inspection area.

106. The States Parties on whose territory transit or basing
points are located shall, as far as possible, assist in
facilitating the inspection, including transporting the
inspection team, its baggage and equipment to the
inspection area, as well as providing the relevant amenities
specified in paragraph 11. The Organization shall
reimburse assisting States Parties for all costs incurred.

107. Subject to the approval of the Executive Council, the
Director-General may negotiate standing arrangements with

States Parties to facilitate assistance in the event of an onsite inspection in an area beyond the jurisdiction or control of any State.

108. In cases where one or more States Parties have conducted an investigation of an ambiguous event in an area beyond the jurisdiction or control of any State before a request is made for an on-site inspection in that area, any results of such investigation may be taken into account by the Executive Council in its deliberations pursuant to Article IV.

Post-Inspection Procedures

109. Upon conclusion of the inspection, the inspection team shall meet with the representative of the inspected

State Party to review the preliminary findings of the
inspection team and to clarify any ambiguities. The
inspection team shall provide the representative of the
inspected State Party with its preliminary findings in written
form according to a standardized format, together with a list
of any samples and other material taken from the inspection
area pursuant to paragraph 98. The document shall be
signed by the head of the inspection team. In order to
indicate that he or she has taken notice of the contents of
the document, the representative of the inspected State
Party shall countersign the document. The meeting shall be
completed no later than 24 hours after the conclusion of the

inspection.

Departure

110. Upon completion of the post-inspection procedures, the inspection team and the observer shall leave, as soon as possible, the territory of the inspected State Party. The inspected State Party shall do everything in its power to provide assistance and to ensure the safe conduct of the inspection team, equipment and baggage to the point of exit. Unless agreed otherwise by the inspected State Party and the inspection team, the point of exit used shall be the same as the point of entry.

PART III
CONFIDENCE-BUILDING MEASURES

1. Pursuant to Article IV, paragraph 68, each State Party shall, on a voluntary basis, provide the Technical Secretariat with notification of any chemical explosion using 300 tonnes or greater of TNT-equivalent blasting material detonated as a single explosion anywhere on its territory, or at any place under its jurisdiction or control. If possible, such notification shall be provided in advance. Such notification shall include details on location, time, quantity and type of explosive used, as well as on the configuration and intended purpose of the blast.

2. Each State Party shall, on a voluntary basis, as soon as possible after the entry into force of this Treaty provide to

the Technical Secretariat, and at annual intervals thereafter
update, information related to its national use of all other
chemical explosions greater than 300 tonnes TNTequivalent.
In particular, the State Party shall seek to advise:
(a) The geographic locations of sites where the explosions originate;
(b) The nature of activities producing them and the
general profile and frequency of such explosions;
(c) Any other relevant detail, if available; and to assist the Technical Secretariat in clarifying the origins of
any such event detected by the International Monitoring System.
3. A State Party may, on a voluntary and mutually

acceptable basis, invite representatives of the Technical Secretariat or of other States Parties to visit sites within its territory referred to in paragraphs 1 and 2.

4. For the purpose of calibrating the International Monitoring System, States Parties may liaise with the Technical Secretariat to carry out chemical calibration explosions or to provide relevant information on chemical explosions planned for other purposes.

ANNEX 1 TO THE PROTOCOL

Table 1-A List of Seismological Stations Comprising the Primary Network

	State Responsible for Station	Location	Latitude	Longitude	Type
1	Argentina	PLCA	40.7 S	70.6 W	3-C

Paso Flores
2 Australia WRA 19.9 S 134.3 E array Warramunga, NT
3 Australia ASAR 23.7 S 133.9 E array Alice Springs, NT
4 Australia STKA 31.9 S 141.6 E 3-C Stephens Creek, SA
5 Australia MAW 67.6 S 62.9 E 3-C Mawson, Antarctica
6 Bolivia LPAZ 16.3 S 68.1 W 3-C La Paz
7 Brazil BDFB 15.6 S 48.0 W 3-C Brasilia
8 Canada ULMC 50.2 N 95.9 W 3-C Lac du Bonnet, Man.
9 Canada YKAC 62.5 N 114.6 W array Yellowknife, N.W.T.
10 Canada SCH 54.8 N 66.8 W 3-C Schefferville, Quebec
11 Central African BGCA 05.2 N 18.4 E 3-C Republic Bangui
12 China HAI 49.3 N 119.7 E 3-C > array Hailar

State Responsible for Station	Location	Latitude	Longitude	Type
13 China	LZH Lanzhou	36.1 N	103.8 E	3-C > array
14 Colombia	XSA El Rosal	04.9 N	74.3 W	3-C
15 Côte d'Ivoire	DBIC Dimbroko	06.7 N	04.9 W	3-C
16 Egypt	LXEG Luxor	26.0 N	33.0 E	array
17 Finland	FINES Lahti	61.4 N	26.1 E	array
18 France	PPT Tahiti	17.6 S	149.6 W	3-C
19 Germany	GEC2 Freyung	48.9 N	13.7 E	array
20 To be determined	To be determined	To be determined	To be determined	To be determined
21 Iran (Islamic Republic of)	THR Tehran	35.8 N	51.4 E	3-C
22 Japan	MJAR Matsushiro	36.5 N	138.2 E	array

	State	Responsible for Station	Location	Latitude	Longitude	Type
22	Kazakstan	MAK Makanchi		46.8 N	82.0 E	array
23	Kenya	KMBO Kilimambogo		01.1 S	37.2 E	3-C
24	Mongolia	JAVM Javhlant		48.0 N	106.8 E	3-C > array
25	Niger	New Site to be determined	to be determined			3-C > array

-161-

	State	Responsible for Station	Location	Latitude	Longitude	Type
26	Norway	NAO Hamar		60.8 N	10.8 E	array
27	Norway	ARAO Karasjok		69.5 N	25.5 E	array
28	Pakistan	PRPK Pari		33.7 N	73.3 E	array
29	Paraguay	CPUP Villa Florida		26.3 S	57.3 W	3-C
30	Republic of Korea	KSRS Wonju		37.5 N	127.9 E	array
31	Russian Federation	KBZ Khabaz		43.7 N	42.9 E	3-C

	State	Responsible for Station	Location	Latitude	Longitude	Type
33	Russian Federation	ZAL Zalesovo	53.9 N	84.8 E	3-C > array
34	Russian Federation	NRI Norilsk	69.0 N	88.0 E	3-C
35	Russian Federation	PDY Peleduy	59.6 N	112.6 E	3-C > array
36	Russian Federation	PET Petropavlovsk-Kamchatskiy	53.1 N	157.8 E	3-C > array
37	Russian Federation	USK Ussuriysk	44.2 N	132.0 E	3-C > array
38	Saudi Arabia	New Site to be determined	to be determined			array
39	South Africa	BOSA Boshof	28.6 S	25.6 E	3-C
40	Spain	ESDC Sonseca	39.7 N	04.0 W	array

41	Thailand	CMTO	18.8 N	99.0 E	array
	Chiang Mai				
42	Tunisia	THA	35.6 N	08.7 E	3-C
	Thala				
43	Turkey	BRTR	39.9 N	32.8 E	array
	Belbashi				
	The array is subject to relocation at Keskin				
44	Turkmenistan	GEYT	37.9 N	58.1 E	array
	Alibeck				
45	Ukraine	AKASG	50.4 N	29.1 E	array
	Malin				
46	United States of America	LJTX Lajitas, TX	29.3 N	103.7 W	array
47	United States of America	MNV Mina, NV	38.4 N	118.2 W	array
48	United States of America	PIWY Pinedale, WY	42.8 N	109.6 W	array
49	United States of America	ELAK Eielson, AK	64.8 N	146.9 W	array
50	United States of America	VNDA Vanda, Antarctica	77.5 S	161.9 E	3-C

Key: 3-C > array: Indicates that the site could start operations in the International

Monitoring System as a three-component station and be upgraded to an array at a later time.

Table 1-B List of Seismological Stations Comprising the Auxiliary Network

State responsible for station		Location	Latitude	Longitude	Type
1	Argentina	CFA Coronel Fontana	31.6 S	68.2 W	3-C
2	Argentina	USHA Ushuaia	55.0 S	68.0 W	3-C
3	Armenia	GNI Garni	40.1 N	44.7 E	3-C
4	Australia	CTA Charters Towers, QLD	20.1 S	146.3 E	3-C
5	Australia	FITZ Fitzroy Crossing, WA	18.1 S	125.6 E	3-C
6	Australia	NWAO Narrogin, WA	32.9 S	117.2 E	3-C

	State responsible for station	Location	Latitude	Longitude	Type
7	Bangladesh	CHT Chittagong	22.4 N	91.8 E	3-C
8	Bolivia	SIV San Ignacio	16.0 S	61.1 W	3-C
9	Botswana	LBTB Lobatse	25.0 S	25.6 E	3-C
10	Brazil	PTGA Pitinga	0.7 S	60.0 W	3-C
11	Brazil	RGNB Rio Grande do Norte	6.9 S	37.0 W	3-C
12	Canada	FRB Iqaluit, N.W.T.	63.7 N	68.5 W	3-C
13	Canada	DLBC Dease Lake, B.C.	58.4 N	130.0 W	3-C
14	Canada	SADO Sadowa, Ont.	44.8 N	79.1 W	3-C
15	Canada	BBB Bella Bella, B.C.	52.2 N	128.1 W	3-C
16	Canada	MBC	76.2 N	119.4 W	3-C

17	Canada	INK	68.3 N	133.5 W	3-C	Mould Bay, N.W.T. Inuvik, N.W.T.
18	Chile	RPN	27.2 S	109.4 W	3-C	Easter Island
19	Chile	LVC	22.6 S	68.9 W	3-C	Limon Verde
20	China	BJT	40.0 N	116.2 E	3-C	Baijiatuan
21	China	KMI	25.2 N	102.8 E	3-C	Kunming
22	China	SSE	31.1 N	121.2 E	3-C	Sheshan
23	China	XAN	34.0 N	108.9 E	3-C	Xi'an

	State responsible for station		Location	Latitude	Longitude	Type
24	Cook Islands	RAR	21.2 S	159.8 W	3-C	Rarotonga
25	Costa Rica	JTS	10.3 N	85.0 W	3-C	Las Juntas de Abangares

26 Czech Republic VRAC 49.3 N 16.6 E 3-C Vranov
27 Denmark SFJ 67.0 N 50.6 W 3-C Søndre Strømfjord, Greenland
28 Djibouti ATD 11.5 N 42.9 E 3-C Arta Tunnel
29 Egypt KEG 29.9 N 31.8 E 3-C Kottamya
30 Ethiopia FURI 8.9 N 38.7 E 3-C Furi
31 Fiji MSVF 17.8 S 178.1 E 3-C Monasavu, Viti Levu
32 France NOUC 22.1 S 166.3 E 3-C Port Laguerre, New Caledonia
33 France KOG 5.2 N 52.7 W 3-C Kourou, French Guiana
34 Gabon BAMB 1.7 S 13.6 E 3-C Bambay

State responsible Location Latitude Longitude Type

for station

35 Germany/South --- 71.7 S 2.9 W 3-C
Africa SANAE Station,
Antarctica
36 Greece IDI 35.3 N 24.9 E 3-C
Anogia, Crete
37 Guatemala RDG 15.0 N 90.5 W 3-C
Rabir
38 Iceland BORG 64.8 N 21.3 W 3-C
Borgarnes
39 To be determined To be determined To be
To be To be
determined determined determined
40 Indonesia PACI 6.5 S 107.0 E 3-C
Cibinong, Jawa
Barat
41 Indonesia JAY 2.5 S 140.7 E 3-C
Jayapura, Irian Jaya
42 Indonesia SWI 0.9 S 131.3 E 3-C
Sorong, Irian Jaya
43 Indonesia PSI 2.7 N 98.9 E 3-C
Parapat, Sumatera
44 Indonesia KAPI 5.0 S 119.8 E 3-C
Kappang, Sulawesi

	State responsible	Location for station	Latitude	Longitude	Type
45	Indonesia	KUG Kupang, Nusatenggara Timur Selatan	10.2 S	123.6 E	3-C
46	Iran (Islamic Republic of)	KRM Kerman	30.3 N	57.1 E	3-C
47	Iran (Islamic Republic of)	MSN Masjed-e-Soleyman	31.9 N	49.3 E	3-C
48	Israel	MBH Eilath	29.8 N	34.9 E	3-C
49	Israel	PARD Parod	32.6 N	35.3 E	array
50	Italy	ENAS Enna, Sicily	37.5 N	14.3 E	3-C
51	Japan	JNU Ohita, Kyushu	33.1 N	130.9 E	3-C
52	Japan	JOW Kunigami, Okinawa	26.8 N	128.3 E	3-C
53	Japan	JHJ	33.1 N	139.8 E	3-C

Hachijojima, Izu Islands
54 Japan JKA 44.1 N 142.6 E 3-C
Kamikawa-asahi, Hokkaido
55 Japan JCJ 27.1 N 142.2 E 3-C
Chichijima, Ogasawara
56 Jordan --- 32.5 N 37.6 E 3-C
Ashqof
57 Kazakstan BRVK 53.1 N 70.3 E array
Borovoye

State responsible for station	Location	Latitude	Longitude	Type

58 Kazakstan KURK 50.7 N 78.6 E array
Kurchatov
59 Kazakstan AKTO 50.4 N 58.0 E 3-C
Aktyubinsk
60 Kyrgyzstan AAK 42.6 N 74.5 E 3-C
Ala-Archa
61 Madagascar TAN 18.9 S 47.6 E 3-C
Antananarivo

62 Mali KOWA 14.5 N 4.0 W 3-C Kowa
63 Mexico TEYM 20.2 N 88.3 W 3-C Tepich, Yucatan
64 Mexico TUVM 18.0 N 94.4 W 3-C Tuzandepeti, Veracruz
65 Mexico LPBM 24.2 N 110.2 W 3-C La Paz, Baja California Sur
66 Morocco MDT 32.8 N 4.6 W 3-C Midelt
67 Namibia TSUM 19.1 S 17.4 E 3-C Tsumeb
68 Nepal EVN 28.0 N 86.8 E 3-C Everest
69 New Zealand EWZ 43.5 S 170.9 E 3-C Erewhon, South Island

State responsible Location Latitude Longitude Type for station

70 New Zealand RAO 29.2 S 177.9 W 3-C

71	New Zealand	URZ	38.3 S	177.1 E	3-C	Raoul Island Urewera, North Island
72	Norway	SPITS	78.2 N	16.4 E	array	Spitsbergen
73	Norway	JMI	70.9 N	8.7 W	3-C	Jan Mayen
74	Oman	WSAR	23.0 N	58.0 E	3-C	Wadi Sarin
75	Papua New Guinea	PMG	9.4 S	147.2 E	3-C	Port Moresby
76	Papua New Guinea	BIAL	5.3 S	151.1 E	3-C	Bialla
77	Peru	CAJP	7.0 S	78.0 W	3-C	Cajamarca
78	Peru	NNA	12.0 S	76.8 W	3-C	Nana
79	Philippines	DAV	7.1 N	125.6 E	3-C	Davao, Mindanao
80	Philippines	TGY	14.1 N	120.9 E	3-C	Tagaytay, Luzon
81	Romania	MLR	45.5 N	25.9 E	3-C	Muntele Rosu

82 Russian Federation KIRV 58.6 N 49.4 E 3-C Kirov

State responsible for station	Location	Latitude	Longitude	Type
83 Russian Federation	Kislovodsk	KIVO 44.0 N	42.7 E	array
84 Russian Federation	Obninsk	OBN 55.1 N	36.6 E	3-C
85 Russian Federation	Arti	ARU 56.4 N	58.6 E	3-C
86 Russian Federation	Seymchan	SEY 62.9 N	152.4 E	3-C
87 Russian Federation	Talaya	TLY 51.7 N	103.6 E	3-C
88 Russian Federation	Yakutsk	YAK 62.0N	129.7 E	3-C
89 Russian Federation	Urgal	URG 51.1N	132.3 E	3-C
90 Russian Federation	Bilibino	BIL 68.0 N	166.4 E	3-C
91 Russian Federation	Tiksi	TIXI 71.6 N	128.9 E	3-C

92	Russian Federation	YSS	47.0 N	142.8 E	3-C	Yuzhno-Sakhalinsk
93	Russian Federation	MA2	59.6 N	150.8 E	3-C	Magadan
94	Russian Federation	ZIL	53.9 N	57.0 E	3-C	Zilim
95	Samoa	AFI	13.9 S	171.8 W	3-C	Afiamalu

	State responsible for station	Location	Latitude	Longitude	Type	
96	Saudi Arabia	RAYN	23.6 N	45.6 E	3-C	Ar Rayn
97	Senegal	MBO	14.4 N	17.0 W	3-C	Mbour
98	Solomon Islands	HNR	9.4 S	160.0 E	3-C	Honiara, Guadalcanal
99	South Africa	SUR	32.4 S	20.8 E	3-C	Sutherland
100	Sri Lanka	COC	6.9 N	79.9 E	3-C	Colombo
101	Sweden	HFS	60.1 N	13.7 E	array	

			Hagfors			
102	Switzerland	DAVOS	Davos	46.8 N	9.8 E	3-C
103	Uganda	MBRU	Mbarara	0.4 S	30.4 E	3-C
104	United Kingdom	EKA	Eskdalemuir	55.3 N	3.2 W	array
105	United States of America	GUMO	Guam, Marianas Islands	13.6 N	144.9 E	3-C
106	United States of America	PMSA	Palmer Station, Antarctica	64.8 S	64.1 W	3-C

-172-

	State responsible for station		Location	Latitude	Longitude	Type
107	United States of America	TKL	Tuckaleechee Caverns, TN	35.7 N	83.8 W	3-C
108	United States of America	PFCA	Piñon Flat, CA	33.6 N	116.5 W	3-C
109	United States of America	YBH	Yreka, CA	41.7 N	122.7 W	3-C

	State responsible	Location		Latitude	Longitude	Type for station
110	United States of America	Kodiak Island, AK	KDC	57.8 N	152.5 W	3-C
111	United States of America	Albuquerque, NM	ALQ	35.0 N	106.5 W	3-C
112	United States of America	Attu Island, AK	ATTU	52.8 N	172.7 E	3-C
113	United States of America	Elko, NV	ELK	40.7 N	115.2 W	3-C
114	United States of America	South Pole, Antarctica	SPA	90.0 S	-	3-C
115	United States of America	Newport, WA	NEW	48.3 N	117.1 W	3-C
116	United States of America	San Juan, PR	SJG	18.1 N	66.2 W	3-C
117	Venezuela	Santo Domingo	SDV	8.9 N	70.6 W	3-C
118	Venezuela	Puerto la Cruz	PCRV	10.2 N	64.6 W	3-C

-173-

	State responsible	Location		Latitude	Longitude	Type for station
119	Zambia	LSZ		15.3 S	28.2 E	3-C

Lusaka

120 Zimbabwe Bulawayo BUL to be advised to be advised 3-C

Table 2-A List of Radionuclide Stations

State responsible for station Location Latitude Longitude

1 Argentina Buenos Aires 34.0 S 58.0 W
2 Argentina Salta 24.0 S 65.0 W
3 Argentina Bariloche 41.1 S 71.3 W
4 Australia Melbourne, VIC 37.5 S 144.6 E
5 Australia Mawson, Antarctica 67.6 S 62.5 E
6 Australia Townsville, QLD 19.2 S 146.8 E
7 Australia Macquarie Island 54.0 S 159.0 E
8 Australia Cocos Islands 12.0 S 97.0 E
9 Australia Darwin, NT 12.4 S 130.7 E
10 Australia Perth, WA 31.9 S 116.0 E
11 Brazil Rio de Janeiro 22.5 S 43.1 W
12 Brazil Recife 8.0 S 35.0 W
13 Cameroon Douala 4.2 N 9.9 E
14 Canada Vancouver, B.C. 49.3 N 123.2 W
15 Canada Resolute, N.W.T. 74.7 N 94.9 W
16 Canada Yellowknife, N.W.T. 62.5 N 114.5 W

17 Canada St. John's, N.L. 47.0 N 53.0 W
18 Chile Punta Arenas 53.1 S 70.6 W
19 Chile Hanga Roa, Easter Island 27.1 S 108.4 W
20 China Beijing 39.8 N 116.2 E
21 China Lanzhou 35.8 N 103.3 E

State responsible for Location Latitude Longitude station

22 China Guangzhou 23.0 N 113.3 E
23 Cook Islands Rarotonga 21.2 S 159.8 W
24 Ecuador Isla San Cristóbal, 1.0 S 89.2 W Galápagos Islands
25 Ethiopia Filtu 5.5 N 42.7 E
26 Fiji Nadi 18.0 S 177.5 E
27 France Papeete, Tahiti 17.0 S 150.0 W
28 France Pointe-à-Pitre, Guadeloupe 17.0 N 62.0 W
29 France Réunion 21.1 S 55.6 E
30 France Port-aux-Français, 49.0 S 70.0 E Kerguelen
31 France Cayenne, French Guiana 5.0 N 52.0 W

32 France Dumont d'Urville, Antarctica 66.0 S 140.0 E
33 Germany Schauinsland/Freiburg 47.9 N 7.9 E
34 Iceland Reykjavik 64.4 N 21.9 W
35 To be determined To be determined To be To be
determined determined
36 Iran (Islamic Republic of) Tehran 35.0 N 52.0 E
37 Japan Okinawa 26.5 N 127.9 E
38 Japan Takasaki, Gunma 36.3 N 139.0 E
39 Kiribati Kiritimati 2.0 N 157.0 W
40 Kuwait Kuwait City 29.0 N 48.0 E
41 Libya Misratah 32.5 N 15.0 E
42 Malaysia Kuala Lumpur 2.6 N 101.5 E

State responsible for Location Latitude Longitude
station

43 Mauritania Nouakchott 18.0 N 17.0 W
44 Mexico Baja California 28.0 N 113.0 W
45 Mongolia Ulaanbaatar 47.5 N 107.0 E
46 New Zealand Chatham Island 44.0 S 176.5 W
47 New Zealand Kaitaia 35.1 S 173.3 E

48 Niger Bilma 18.0 N 13.0 E
49 Norway Spitsbergen 78.2 N 16.4 E
50 Panama Panama City 8.9 N 79.6 W
51 Papua New Guinea New Hanover 3.0 S 150.0 E
52 Philippines Quezon City 14.5 N 121.0 E
53 Portugal Ponta Delgada, São Miguel, 37.4 N 25.4 W
Azores
54 Russian Federation Kirov 58.6 N 49.4 E
55 Russian Federation Norilsk 69.0 N 88.0E
56 Russian Federation Peleduy 59.6 N 112.6 E
57 Russian Federation Bilibino 68.0 N 166.4 E
58 Russian Federation Ussuriysk 43.7 N 131.9 E
59 Russian Federation Zalesovo 53.9 N 84.8 E
60 Russian Federation Petropavlovsk-Kamchatskiy 53.1 N 158.8 E
61 Russian Federation Dubna 56.7 N 37.3 E
62 South Africa Marion Island 46.5 S 37.0 E
63 Sweden Stockholm 59.4 N 18.0 E
64 Tanzania Dar es Salaam 6.0 S 39.0 E
65 Thailand Bangkok 13.8 N 100.5 E

	State responsible for station	Location	Latitude	Longitude
66	United Kingdom	BIOT/Chagos Archipelago	7.0 S	72.0 E
67	United Kingdom	St. Helena	16.0 S	6.0 W
68	United Kingdom	Tristan da Cunha	37.0 S	12.3 W
69	United Kingdom	Halley, Antarctica	76.0 S	28.0 W
70	United States of America	Sacramento, CA	38.7 N	121.4 W
71	United States of America	Sand Point, AK	55.0 N	160.0 W
72	United States of America	Melbourne, FL	28.3 N	80.6 W
73	United States of America	Palmer Station, Antarctica	64.5 S	64.0 W
74	United States of America	Ashland, KS	37.2 N	99.8 W
75	United States of America	Charlottesville, VA	38.0 N	78.0 W
76	United States of America	Salchaket, AK	64.4 N	147.1 W

77 United States of America Wake Island 19.3 N 166.6 E
78 United States of America Midway Islands 28.0 N 177.0 W
79 United States of America Oahu, HI 21.5 N 158.0 W
80 United States of America Upi, Guam 13.7 N 144.9 E

Table 2-B List of Radionuclide Laboratories

State	Name and place of laboratory responsible for Laboratory
1 Argentina	National Board of Nuclear Regulation, Buenos Aires
2 Australia	Australian Radiation Laboratory, Melbourne, VIC
3 Austria	Austrian Research Center Seibersdorf
4 Brazil	Institute of Radiation Protection and Dosimetry, Rio de Janeiro
5 Canada	Health Canada

Ottawa, Ont.
6 China Beijing
7 Finland Centre for Radiation and Nuclear Safety
Helsinki
8 France Atomic Energy Commission
Montlhéry
9 Israel Soreq Nuclear Research Centre
Yavne

State	Name and place of laboratory responsible for Laboratory
10 Italy	Laboratory of the National Agency for the Protection of the Environment Rome
11 Japan	Japan Atomic Energy Research Institute Tokai, Ibaraki
12 New Zealand	National Radiation Laboratory Christchurch
13 Russian Federation	Central Radiation Control Laboratory, Ministry of Defence Special Verification Service Moscow

1	South Africa	Atomic Energy Corporation		
4		Pelindaba		
1	United Kingdom	AWE Blacknest		
5		Chilton		
1	United States of America	McClellan Central Laboratories		
6		Sacramento, CA		

-180-

Table 3 List of Hydroacoustic Stations

	State responsible for station	Location	Latitude	Longitude	Type
1	Australia	Cape Leeuwin, WA	34.4 S	115.1 E	Hydrophone
2	Canada	Queen Charlotte Islands, B.C.	53.3 N	132.5 W	T-phase
3	Chile	Juan Fernández Island	33.7 S	78.8 W	Hydrophone
4	France	Crozet Islands	46.5 S	52.2 E	Hydrophone
5	France	Guadeloupe	16.3 N	61.1 W	T-phase
6	Mexico	Clarión Island	18.2 N	114.6 W	T-phase

	State responsible for station	Location	Latitude	Longitude	Type
7	Portugal	Flores	39.3 N	31.3 W	T-phase
8	United Kingdom	BIOT/Chagos Archipelago	7.3 S	72.4 E	Hydrophone
9	United Kingdom	Tristan da Cunha	37.2 S	12.5 W	T-phase
10	United Kingdom	Ascension	8.0 S	14.4 W	Hydrophone
11	United States of America	Wake Island	19.3 N	166.6 E	Hydrophone

Table 4 List of Infrasound Stations

	State responsible for station	Location	Latitude	Longitude
1	Argentina	Paso Flores	40.7 S	70.6 W
2	Argentina	Ushuaia	55.0 S	68.0 W
3	Australia	Davis Base, Antarctica	68.4 S	77.6 E
4	Australia	Narrogin, WA	32.9 S	117.2 E
5	Australia	Hobart, TAS	42.1 S	147.2 E

	State responsible for station	Location	Latitude	Longitude
6	Australia	Cocos Islands	12.3 S	97.0 E
7	Australia	Warramunga, NT	19.9 S	134.3 E
8	Bolivia	La Paz	16.3 S	68.1 W
9	Brazil	Brasilia	15.6 S	48.0 W
10	Canada	Lac du Bonnet, Man.	50.2 N	95.9 W
11	Cape Verde	Cape Verde Islands	16.0 N	24.0 W
12	Central African Republic	Bangui	5.2 N	18.4 E
13	Chile	Easter Island	27.0 S	109.2 W
14	Chile	Juan Fernández Island	33.8 S	80.7 W
15	China	Beijing	40.0 N	116.0 E
16	China	Kunming	25.0 N	102.8 E
17	Côte d'Ivoire	Dimbokro	6.7 N	4.9 W

State responsible for station	Location	Latitude	Longitude
18 Denmark	Dundas, Greenland	76.5 N	68.7 W
19 Djibouti	Djibouti	11.3 N	43.5 E
20 Ecuador	Galápagos Islands	0.0 N	91.7 W

-184-

State responsible for station	Location	Latitude	Longitude
21 France	Marquesas Islands	10.0 S	140.0 W
22 France	Port LaGuerre, New Caledonia	22.1 S	166.3 E
23 France	Kerguelen	49.2 S	69.1 E
24 France	Tahiti	17.6 S	149.6 W
25 France	Kourou, French Guiana	5.2 N	52.7 W
26 Germany	Freyung	48.9 N	13.7 E
27 Germany	Georg von Neumayer, Antarctica	70.6 S	8.4 W

State responsible for station	Location	Latitude	Longitude		
28	To be determined	To be determined	To be determine	To be determined	
29	Iran (Islamic Republic of)	Tehran	35.7 N	51.4 E	
30	Japan	Tsukuba	36.0 N	140.1 E	
31	Kazakstan	Aktyubinsk	50.4 N	58.0 E	
32	Kenya	Kilimanbogo	1.3 S	36.8 E	
33	Madagascar	Antananarivo	18.8 S	47.5 E	
34	Mongolia	Javhlant	48.0 N	106.8 E	
35	Namibia	Tsumeb	19.1 S	17.4 E	
36	New Zealand	Chatham Island	44.0 S	176.5 W	
3	Norway	Karasjok	69.5 N	25.5 E	

State responsible for station	Location	Latitude	Longitude
37	Pakistan	Rahimyar Khan	28.2 N	70.3 E
38	Palau	Palau	7.5 N	134.5 E
39	Papua New Guinea	Rabaul	4.1 S	152.1 E
40	Paraguay	Villa Florida	26.3 S	57.3 W
41	Portugal	Azores	37.8 N	25.5 W
42	Russian Federation	Dubna	56.7 N	37.3 E
43	Russian Federation	Petropavlovsk-Kamchatskiy	53.1 N	158.8 E
44	Russian Federation	Ussuriysk	43.7 N	131.9 E
45	Russian Federation	Zalesovo	53.9 N	84.8 E

State responsible for station	Location	Latitude	Longitude
47	South Africa	Boshof	28.6 S	25.4 E
48	Tunisia	Thala	35.6 N	8.7 E
49	United Kingdom	Tristan da Cunha	37.0 S	12.3 W
50	United Kingdom	Ascension	8.0 S	14.3 W
51	United Kingdom	Bermuda	32.0 N	64.5 W
52	United Kingdom	BIOT/Chagos Archipelago	5.0 S	72.0 E
53	United States of America	Eielson, AK	64.8 N	146.9 W
54	United States of America	Siple Station, Antarctica	75.5 S	83.6 W
55	United States of America	Windless Bight, Antarctica	77.5 S	161.8 E

State Location Latitude Longitude responsible for station

5 United States Newport, WA 48.3 N 117.1 W
6 of America
5 United States Piñon Flat, CA 33.6 N 116.5 W
7 of America
5 United States Midway Islands 28.1N 177.2 W
8 of America
5 United States Hawaii, HI 19.6 N 155.3 W
9 of America
6 United States Wake Island 19.3 N 166.6 E
0 of America

ANNEX 2 TO THE PROTOCOL

List of Characterization Parameters for International Data Centre Standard Event Screening

1. The International Data Centre standard event screening criteria shall be based on the standard event characterization parameters determined during the

combined processing of data from all the monitoring
technologies in the International Monitoring System.
Standard event screening shall make use of both global and
supplementary screening criteria to take account of regional
variations where applicable.

2. For events detected by the International Monitoring
System seismic component, the following parameters, inter
alia, may be used:
- location of the event;
- depth of the event;
- ratio of the magnitude of surface waves to body
waves;
- signal frequency content;
- spectral ratios of phases;
- spectral scalloping;
- first motion of the P-wave;

- focal mechanism;
- relative excitation of seismic phases;
- comparative measures to other events and groups of
events; and
- regional discriminants where applicable.

3. For events detected by the International Monitoring
System hydroacoustic component, the following parameters, inter alia, may be used:
- signal frequency content including corner frequency,
wide-band energy, and mean centre frequency and
bandwidth;
- frequency-dependent duration of signals;
- spectral ratio; and
- indications of bubble-pulse signals and bubble-pulse
delay.

4. For events detected by the International Monitoring

System infrasound component, the following parameters,
inter alia, may be used:
- signal frequency content and dispersion;
- signal duration; and
- peak amplitude.

5. For events detected by the International Monitoring
System radionuclide component, the following parameters,
inter alia, may be used:
- concentration of background natural and man-made
radionuclides;
- concentration of specific fission and activation products outside normal observations; and
- ratios of one specific fission and activation product to
another.

www.ingramcontent.com/pod-product-compliance
Lightning Source LLC
Chambersburg PA
CBHW051622170526
45167CB00001B/26